God's Promises

NEW EVERY DAY

God's Promises
NEW EVERY DAY

A DAILY DEVOTIONAL
STEWART CUSTER

BJU PRESS
GREENVILLE, SOUTH CAROLINA

Cover image by Digital Vision

The fact that materials produced by other publishers may be referred to in this volume does not constitute an endorsement by BJU Press of the content or theological position of materials produced by such publishers. The position of BJU Press, and Bob Jones University itself, is well known. Any references and ancillary materials are listed as an aid to the student or the teacher and in an attempt to maintain the accepted academic standards of the publishing industry.

All Scripture is quoted from the Authorized King James Version unless otherwise specified.

God's Promises New Every Day
Stewart Custer

Design by Micah Ellis
Composition by Melissa Matos

© 2004 BJU Press
Greenville, South Carolina 29614

Printed in the United States of America

ISBN 1-59166-328-8

15 14 13 12 11 10 9 8 7 6 5 4 3 2

Thy words were found,
and I did eat them;
and thy word was unto me
the joy and rejoicing of mine heart:
for I am called by thy name,
O Lord God of hosts.

Jeremiah 15:16

January 1

"*I*n the beginning God . . ." (Gen. 1:1). Begin with God. He is the Origin of all life and light. Every lesser quest ends in failure, but those who seek the Lord find Him. "The young lions do lack, and suffer hunger: but they that seek the Lord shall not want any good thing" (Ps. 34:10). God can satisfy the deepest needs of the human soul. The fiercest animal hunters sometimes go hungry, but the people who seek God are abundantly satisfied. God can impart the serene peace of His presence to your inmost soul. The wars may rage around you, but God can still your heart with His comforting presence. Shooting stars may fall from heaven, but God will never change. He welcomes the seeking soul.

Golden thought: **Those who seek the Lord find Him.**

"The fear of the Lord is the beginning of wisdom" (Ps. 111:10).

January 2

"And I will put enmity between thee and the woman, and between thy seed and her seed; it shall bruise thy head, and thou shalt bruise his heel" (Gen. 3:15). These words to the serpent in the Garden of Eden give the whole plan of salvation. There will be age-long strife between the Devil and mankind. The seed of the woman is a reference to the virgin-born Son of God, the Lord Jesus Christ, whose hands and feet were pierced on the cross for our salvation. His death on the cross was the atoning sacrifice that makes possible the salvation of any who call upon Him. He shall defeat the Devil and gather His saints to Himself. This "first Gospel" is the promise of victory to all who trust in Christ for their eternal salvation. All the promises of God are fulfilled in Him.

_____

Golden thought: **There is victory in Jesus.**

"For whatsoever is born of God overcometh the world: and this is the victory that overcometh the world, even our faith" (I John 5:4).

January 3

"After these things the word of the Lord came unto Abram in a vision, saying, Fear not, Abram: I am thy shield, and thy exceeding great reward" (Gen. 15:1). Abraham had risked his life to rescue his nephew, Lot, from the army of the kings. He had given away the spoils of war rather than getting anything from the wicked king of Sodom. Now God reassures him that He has been watching and is pleased. God is his protection and his reward. The presence of God is still with His people. God alone is our Protector and Deliverer. We should not be discouraged by weariness or danger. God is fully able to take care of His people. We need to depend on His almighty protection.

Golden thought: **God is our shield and our exceeding great reward.**

"Commit thy way unto the Lord; trust also in him; and he shall bring it to pass" (Ps. 37:5).

January 4

"*O* taste and see that the Lord is good: blessed is the man that trusteth in him" (Ps. 34:8). The psalmist uses the experience of taste to invite us to have a stronger relationship with God. The person who trusts in God will discover that He is much greater and much more compassionate to His people than he has yet experienced. The title of the psalm shows that David had been one step away from death when he was delivered. He could say, "This poor man cried, and the Lord heard him, and saved him out of all his troubles" (Ps. 34:6). We, too, need to cry to the Lord for help and deliverance in time of need. We will experience the greatness of His presence and protection with us.

Golden thought: **Blessed is the person who trusts in God.**
"Many are the afflictions of the righteous: but the Lord delivereth him out of them all" (Ps. 34:19).

January 5

"Ask, and it shall be given you; seek, and ye shall find; knock, and it shall be opened unto you" (Matt. 7:7). There is an ascending seriousness in these three commands. All three are present tense imperatives, literally, "Keep on asking; keep on seeking; keep on knocking." The believer must earnestly direct his thoughts toward God and not allow the things of this world to distract him from such a high quest. Every believer should persevere in prayer. Seeking God is the highest purpose a human being can have. Knocking on the door of heaven is the most important task that we have. That God should be pleased to hear from us is an astonishing thought. "Enter into his gates with thanksgiving" (Ps. 100:4).

Golden thought: **Ask, seek, knock; He is listening.**
"For every one that asketh receiveth; and he that seeketh findeth; and to him that knocketh it shall be opened" (Matt. 7:8).

January 6

"*B*ut my God shall supply all your need according to his riches in glory by Christ Jesus" (Phil. 4:19). The apostle Paul could speak out of a long experience of God's gracious provision. God is not concerned about the many fleeting desires that we may have, but He is seriously concerned about the real needs of our heart. God promises to meet all of our serious needs, not in a feeble, earthly way, but according to His riches in glory. God has abundant provision for the needs of the human heart. All our needs can be met in Christ Jesus. He is God's abundant provision for our desperate needs. We need to seek the Lord Jesus Christ for the provision of grace that He can impart to every one of us.

Golden thought: **"God shall supply all your need."**
"Rejoice in the Lord alway: and again I say, Rejoice" (Phil. 4:4).

January 7

"*T*he Lord is my light and my salvation; whom shall I fear? the Lord is the strength of my life; of whom shall I be afraid?" (Ps. 27:1). Fear has no place in the life of one who trusts in the Lord Jesus Christ. He has all the power we need. He is the light of this dark world. He is our eternal salvation. We may easily lose our physical strength, but the Lord has inexhaustible strength for His people. There is no circumstance of life that can intimidate Him. "Who can break the vessel that the Lord intends to use again?" (Spurgeon). Our lives should radiate the light of the Lord. Our confidence in His keeping power should be manifest to all who know us.

————————————

Golden thought: **"The Lord is the strength of my life."**
"Though an host should encamp against me, my heart shall not fear" (Ps. 27:3).

January 8

"God is our refuge and strength, a very present help in trouble" (Ps. 46:1). At times, trials and problems come thick and fast. The believer may be tempted to panic, but there is always one calming thought: God is never surprised or disturbed. We may flee to Him for refuge and protection. He can impart to us all the strength and wisdom we need. When trouble comes, He is always there to help us. No wonder that the psalmist was so confident: "Therefore will not we fear, though the earth be removed, and though the mountains be carried into the midst of the sea" (Ps. 46:2). God is sufficient for every emergency we will ever encounter. "The Lord of hosts is with us" (Ps. 46:7).

Golden thought: **"God is our refuge and strength."**
"Be still, and know that I am God" (Ps. 46:10).

January 9

"*If* any of you lack wisdom, let him ask of God, that giveth to all men liberally, and upbraideth not; and it shall be given him" (James 1:5). If there is one thing believers are sure of, it is that they have already acted foolishly enough for a lifetime! We all need to ask God for wisdom so that we may live in a way that honors Him. Wisdom is a great gift of the Spirit of God (I Cor. 12:8). Solomon asked the Lord for wisdom to rule his people rightly (I Kings 3:5–9). The Lord was so pleased that He not only gave him wisdom but also gave him a great deal more that he had not asked for (I Kings 3:12–14). It is Christ Jesus "who of God is made unto us wisdom" (I Cor. 1:30). There is no excuse for us to act foolishly.

Golden thought: **If you lack wisdom, ask God for it.**

"Christ the power of God, and the wisdom of God" (I Cor. 1:24).

January 10

"Peace I leave with you, my peace I give unto you: not as the world giveth, give I unto you. Let not your heart be troubled, neither let it be afraid" (John 14:27). The world is in such chaos that peace is almost nonexistent. Even believers often find themselves in a harried and troubled state of mind. Rather than just gritting their teeth, believers should remember that the Lord Jesus is the source of true peace. We must trust the Lord Jesus to fill our hearts with the serene peace of His gracious presence. Part of the fruit of the Spirit is peace (Gal. 5:22). The Lord Jesus is a wonderful example of this grace. In the midst of chaos He was always conscious of His Father's presence (John 8:16).

Golden thought: **"My peace I give unto you."**
On the day of His resurrection Jesus said, "Peace be unto you" (John 20:19).

January 11

"Come unto me, all ye that labour and are heavy laden, and I will give you rest" (Matt. 11:28). Many people are bowed down and exhausted, struggling under a load they cannot carry. The Lord Jesus Christ invites all who so labor to come to Him. He is able to lift the burden, to impart strength to the weary. We should stop struggling to accomplish our purposes and let Him accomplish His purpose through us. He will give us rest because He will work through us to bring about His perfect will. We will not have to prove how good we are; we can point to Him and show men how great He is. He invites us, "Take my yoke upon you and learn of me; for I am meek and lowly in heart: and ye shall find rest unto your souls" (v. 29).

Golden thought: **Jesus says, "I will give you rest."**
"In returning and rest shall ye be saved" (Isa. 30:15).

January 12

"*B*ehold, the Lord's hand is not shortened, that it cannot save; neither his ear heavy, that it cannot hear" (Isa. 59:1). The Bible clearly tells us that God is always able to deliver His people. If we have a sense that He is not listening to us, it is because sin has distracted us from fellowship with Him. "But your iniquities have separated between you and your God" (Isa. 59:2). We need to ask Him to forgive us and to restore us to fellowship with Him. The blood of the Lord Jesus Christ covers every sin. We need to plead the blood and bring ourselves back into fellowship with God. Then He can answer our prayers and guide our steps according to His perfect will.

———————————

Golden thought: **God is near; He is listening.**

God says, "My words which I have put in thy mouth, shall not depart out of thy mouth" (Isa. 59:21).

January 13

"*The* eyes of the Lord run to and fro throughout the whole earth, to show himself strong in behalf of them whose heart is perfect toward him" (II Chron. 16:9). The seer Hanani rebuked King Asa because he relied on the king of Syria instead of the Lord God. We are all tempted to rely upon people instead of God. But God is always searching for people who will trust Him rather than men. You cannot put your trust in God without His being aware of it. God is delighted to uphold the people who are right with Him. Putting yourself in the center of God's will and trusting Him is the safest place in the world for you as a believer. But believers must be careful to base their conduct on the revealed Word of God.

Golden thought: **God is watching to show Himself strong in behalf of His people.**

"O my God, I trust in thee: let me not be ashamed" (Ps. 25:2).

January 14

"For whosoever hath, to him shall be given, and he shall have more abundance: but whosoever hath not, from him shall be taken away even that he hath" (Matt. 13:12). The Lord Jesus speaks here concerning spiritual truth in His Word: to the person who has even a little of it, God desires to add much more. But if the person does not have God's truth, he will lose even the little spiritual perception that he has. There are religious fanatics in the world. But if a person has even a small perception of what the Bible teaches, God desires to illuminate much more to him. God desires to fill the believer with spiritual perception. We need to ask Him for spiritual light and understanding of His holy Word.

Golden thought: **If you understand part of the Bible, God is ready to illuminate more.**

"Open thou mine eyes, that I may behold wondrous things out of thy law" (Ps. 119:18).

January 15

"*T*hou wilt keep him in perfect peace, whose mind is stayed on thee: because he trusteth in thee" (Isa. 26:3). Only the Lord God could give such a promise because only He has the power to impart such perfect peace. The believer often has the task of fighting fierce battles, against terrible odds. If he stands alone, he will go down in defeat. If he will just trust the Lord, he will gain the victory. We need to keep our thoughts stayed upon Him. As we think about His power and His promises, the enemies will become smaller and smaller. We must not be intimidated by midgets when we have the Lord of all on our side. Think about Him!

Golden thought: **God promises "perfect peace."**
"Trust ye in the Lord for ever: for in the Lord JEHOVAH is everlasting strength" (Isa. 26:4).

January 16

"The eyes of the Lord are over the righteous, and his ears are open unto their prayers" (I Pet. 3:12). There are times when the believer feels abandoned. His prayers seem to be unheeded, and he is getting deeper into trouble. That is the time that the believer needs to remember this promise. God is watching; He hears every prayer. But God is also supremely wise. He knows exactly how to deliver His people and the perfect time in which to work His will. Believers tend to panic if the answer does not come quickly. We need to learn to trust the Lord. He will do exactly what is right. He never forgets His people. We must walk humbly with Him and obey His Word, for He is leading us homeward. ─────────────

Golden thought: **God is listening.**

"And who is he that will harm you, if ye be followers of that which is good?" (I Pet. 3:13).

January 17

"*T*he Lord is thy keeper: the Lord is thy shade upon thy right hand" (Ps. 121:5). At times the believer may find himself in difficult or even dangerous circumstances. He should always remember that his life does not depend on his wits but on the keeping power of his God. If the Lord is keeping you, you may relax. God does not forget you and cannot make a mistake. His presence with you is your protection. But He does not merely protect you; He is your shade from the burning sun. In the hot and dry Holy Land that had special meaning. God provides comfort for the believer that he often takes for granted. We should remind ourselves to thank God for blessings great and small.

Golden thought: **The Lord is your keeper.**
"He that keepeth thee will not slumber" (Ps. 121:3).

January 18

"The Lord shall preserve thee from all evil: he shall preserve thy soul" (Ps. 121:7). God preserves the believer from all that would harm his soul. He does not preserve him from discipline or chastisement that would improve his eternal well being. Believers often ask God for better circumstances, but those circumstances would often harm them, or hinder their service. God is training the believer to be an eternal servant for Him. A difficult pathway is often part of the training. Nothing that harms the eternal relationship with God will be allowed into his life. If the believer steps away from God, he alone is responsible for the consequences. God desires the best for him.

Golden thought: **"The Lord shall preserve thee from all evil."**
"My help cometh from the Lord" (Ps. 121:2).

January 19

"The Lord shall preserve thy going out and thy coming in from this time forth, and even for evermore" (Ps. 121:8). God's hand of preservation is especially upon believers when they must venture forth into new surroundings. Whether it is moving to a new location or venturing into a new activity, the believer should be aware that God's hand of blessing rests upon him. But God is especially interested in bringing the believer safely home. Not only does God bring the believer safely to his earthly home but He will also bring him safely to his eternal home that He has been preparing for him. The celestial city of Revelation 21 is the eternal home that God is preparing for every true believer in Christ.

Golden thought: **"The Lord shall preserve thy going out and thy coming in."**
"He that keepeth thee will not slumber" (Ps. 121:3).

January 20

"Wherefore come out from among them, and be ye separate, saith the Lord, and touch not the unclean thing; and I will receive you, and will be a Father unto you, and ye shall be my sons and daughters, saith the Lord Almighty" (II Cor. 6:17–18). Believers in Christ must turn their backs upon idols, false religions, evil companions, and anything else that would draw them away from Christ. There is no communion possible between light and darkness (II Cor. 6:14). If you walk in the light, darkness must flee. Believers should never regret giving up things or people that drag them downward. Being a child of the Almighty King is more important than anything else in the world.

Golden thought: **"Be ye separate . . . and I will receive you."**
"Having these promises, dearly beloved, let us cleanse ourselves from all filthiness of the flesh and spirit, perfecting holiness in the fear of God" (II Cor. 7:1).

January 21

"*H*e hath said, I will never leave thee, nor forsake thee" (Heb. 13:5). Therefore, our manner of life ought to be without covetousness. We have the Lord of the universe with us at all times. He will certainly supply us with all we need. There is no circumstance of life so difficult, or so dangerous, that He cannot deal with it. Fair weather friends may abandon us, but God will never leave us. That assurance ought to make us better servants of the Lord. If He is always with us, we ought to serve with cheerfulness and diligence. To please Him should be the happiest task in our lives. If we must face enemies, it ought to be with the confidence that God is able to accomplish His purpose though us.

Golden thought: **God says, "I will never leave thee, nor forsake thee."**

"So that we may boldly say, The Lord is my helper, and I will not fear what man shall do unto me" (Heb. 13:6).

January 22

"*I*f any man sin, we have an advocate with the Father, Jesus Christ the righteous" (I John 2:1). Even strong believers sometimes stumble into sin. If that should happen, no believer should just lie there in the mire. He should at once plead for rescue by his great Savior, the Lord Jesus Christ. He is our Advocate, the one who pleads our cause in the courts of heaven. He is the Righteous One, whose death upon the cross atones for the sins of the world. We can ask for forgiveness and cleansing by the blood of the Lamb. His will for us is that we avoid sin, but if we should sin, His provision for us is infinite. Let us walk humbly with Him, letting Him guide our steps that we may avoid sin.

Golden thought: **"We have an advocate . . . Jesus Christ the righteous."**

"My little children, these things write I unto you, that ye sin not" (I John 2:1).

January 23

"*H*im that cometh to me I will in no wise cast out" (John 6:37). The Lord Jesus spoke this promise to a crowd that was by no means sure of who He was. But He offers welcome to anyone who will come to Him. By faith we may come boldly to Him, knowing that He will forgive the sinful, cleanse the defiled, strengthen the weak, and transform His people into all that they should be for Him. He desires us to come to Him because He is the only one who can meet our needs and make us good servants of God. He is the Lord of all, who can take humble people and make them instruments of blessing by His grace and power. Let us seek His face in humble submission.

Golden thought: **Come; He will in no wise cast us out.**

Jesus said, "He that cometh to me shall never hunger" (John 6:35).

January 24

"*F*or the joy of the Lord is your strength" (Neh. 8:10). Ezra the scribe had read the law of the Lord to the people, and they had wept when they perceived how disobedient they had been (Neh. 8:8–9). But a day of repentance and renewal is not a time for sorrow. Nehemiah encouraged the people, for now they desired to do the will of the Lord. A time of rededication is a time for rejoicing. The person who knows the Lord Jesus Christ as Savior should not go around with a morose attitude, even if he is convicted of his sins. The Lord Jesus died to provide forgiveness. The believer should rejoice in the mercy and grace of God. The joy of the Lord is his strength to live for Him this day.

Golden thought: **"The joy of the Lord is your strength."**
"Rejoice in the Lord alway: and again I say, Rejoice" (Phil. 4:4).

January 25

"*C*ommit thy works unto the Lord, and thy thoughts shall be established" (Prov. 16:3). The person who thinks that he must serve the Lord in his own strength is doomed to failure. No one can serve the Lord well in his own strength. But if the believer trusts the Lord to supply to him the wisdom and strength that he needs, he will discover that the Lord does impart to him all that he needs to serve Him well. Serving in the strength of the Lord imparts great peace and serenity to the believer. His thoughts are established because he does not have to cast about desperately to know how to serve. God imparts His wisdom to the believer that he may walk pleasing to the Lord.

Golden thought: **"Thy thoughts shall be established."**
"A man's heart deviseth his way: but the Lord directeth his steps" (Prov. 16:9).

January 26

"And let us not be weary in well doing: for in due season we shall reap, if we faint not" (Gal. 6:9). Paul urges believers to sow systematically to the Spirit, not to the flesh (Gal. 6:8). Whoever sows to the flesh will reap spiritual disaster. The believer should constantly be sowing thoughts, words, and deeds under the influence of the Spirit of God. There will be a harvest of blessing. The farmer who sows good grain knows he will get a good harvest. But he also knows that he must keep weeding and cultivating the crop. In the same way the believer must keep sowing and cultivating the Word of God that there might be a good harvest in his own life and in the lives of those he ministers to. God is the Lord of the harvest.

Golden thought: **"In due season we shall reap."**

"As we have therefore opportunity, let us do good unto all men, especially unto them who are of the household of faith" (Gal. 6:10).

January 27

"When Christ, who is our life, shall appear, then shall ye also appear with him in glory" (Col. 3:4). The believer should have his mind fixed on things above, not on the property or possessions he may have in this life. They will all pass away, but the glory that he will one day have with the Lord will be eternal. Our affection should be set on the Lord, not on things. Paul goes on to urge the believer to mortify, or put to death, the evil desires he may have (v. 5). His mind should dwell on higher things. There cannot be a higher thought than that of the blessed Lord Himself. We should let our minds dwell deeply on the thought that one day we shall share the glories of heaven with Him.

Golden thought: **You shall appear with Him in glory.**

"And let the peace of God rule in your hearts" (Col. 3:15).

January 28

"*B*ut love ye your enemies, and do good, and lend, hoping for nothing again; and your reward shall be great, and ye shall be the children of the Highest: for he is kind unto the unthankful and to the evil" (Luke 6:35). Rather than being known as a "hard-nosed dealer," the believer should be known as a kind and considerate person. There should be a "family resemblance" between God and His children. That does not mean that the believer should be an easy mark for every crook, but it does mean that he cares for others and is patient with them. The believer's life is always an indication of the kind of God he serves. We serve the infinitely kind Father of the Lord Jesus Christ.

Golden thought: **You shall be the children of the Highest.**

"Be ye therefore merciful, as your Father also is merciful" (Luke 6:36).

January 29

"The Lord is good, a strong hold in the day of trouble; and he knoweth them that trust in him" (Nah. 1:7). Nahum warned wicked Nineveh of the Lord's power to judge sin (Nah. 1:2). But the Lord has infinite compassion and mercy upon His people. He is a fortress of protection for those who reverence Him. In the day of trouble His people should flee to Him for refuge. They should never fear, for He knows each one who puts his trust in Him. The God who can dry up the sea and make the mountains quake (vv. 4–5) certainly has the power to deliver His people from any danger that confronts them. We need to trust in the Lord with all our hearts.

Golden thought: **The Lord is a stronghold in the day of trouble.**

In the day of trouble Asaph sought the Lord (Ps. 77:2) and concluded, "Thou art the God that doest wonders" (Ps. 77:14).

January 30

"*H*im that overcometh will I make a pillar in the temple of my God, and he shall go no more out" (Rev. 3:12). God has prepared a marvelous future for His saints. In this life they may be persecuted and hounded from place to place, but in the place that God has prepared for His people in heaven they will never be moved. They will be like a pillar in the temple of God: a figure of adornment and beauty as well as stability. They will never be moved from the presence of God. That is all the more reason for believers to remain steadfast for the Lord in this wicked world. The "overcomer" refers to the true believer who perseveres to the end. God cherishes such a testimony.

Golden thought: **God will make the overcomer a pillar in His temple.**

It is worth the trials and struggles to keep the word of His patience (Rev. 3:10).

January 31

"*D*raw nigh to God, and he will draw nigh to you" (James 4:8). The person who seeks after God in his heart shall find Him. God is looking for such people and will satisfy their longing for Him. The closer the believer draws to God, the closer God draws to the believer. But the person who draws near to God must cleanse and purify himself for God is holy. The person who is prepared to humble himself before God will find that God is ready to lift him up (James 4:10). It is the Lord Jesus Christ Himself who is the way to God. The blood of Jesus is the "new and living way" to God (Heb. 10:20). We may draw near to God "in full assurance of faith" (Heb. 10:22) because of the death of Jesus upon the cross.

Golden thought: **He will draw near to you.**

"Humble yourselves in the sight of the Lord, and he shall lift you up" (James 4:10).

February 1

"*D*elight thyself also in the Lord; and he shall give thee the desires of thine heart" (Ps. 37:4). Our relationship with God should never be just routine. We should delight ourselves in the presence of God, just as we would delight in the visit of a dear friend. He cares for us and has done more for us than any human being ever could. We should look forward to our times of prayer as very special occasions. In the process of such fellowship with God, we will discover that He has answered our inmost longings for specific things. God delights in blessing His children. We should delight in seasons of refreshing in His presence. To talk with a dear friend is always a delight.

Golden thought: **He will give you the desires of your heart.**
"The Lord knoweth the days of the upright; and their inheritance shall be for ever" (Ps. 37:18).

February 2

"Commit thy way unto the Lord; trust also in him; and he shall bring it to pass" (Ps. 37:5). Our best laid plans often fail. God alone knows all the aspects of our life perfectly. We should put our plans into the hands of God and let Him work out His perfect will in them all. We should trust in His divine wisdom to lead us in the best pathway. We do not walk blindly, stumbling along, but trustingly, depending on God to illumine our pathway and to direct our steps according to His perfect will. When we trust Him, we will discover that He has prepared the way before us and guided us into a pathway of blessing that only He could choose. His way is always perfect.

Golden thought: **"He shall bring it to pass."**
"The steps of a good man are ordered by the Lord: and he delighteth in his way" (Ps. 37:23).

February 3

"*For* evildoers shall be cut off: but those that wait upon the Lord, they shall inherit the earth" (Ps. 37:9). Instead of frantically struggling, the believer should rest in the Lord's keeping power (v. 7). The Lord will accomplish all His purpose. It may not be in the manner or the time that the believer expects, but He will work all things out for the believer's eternal benefit. Patient waiting is one of the hardest things that the believer is called upon to do. We are always inclined to rush in and to get everything done at once. But the Almighty is planning the lives of all His people and making all events fit in with His purpose. We cannot hurry that, and we certainly cannot give Him advice.

Golden thought: **"Those that wait upon the Lord . . . shall inherit the earth."**

"A little that a righteous man hath is better than the riches of many wicked" (Ps. 37:16).

February 4

"*F*or we know that if our earthly house of this tabernacle were dissolved, we have a building of God, an house not made with hands, eternal in the heavens" (II Cor. 5:1). The "earthly house" (literally, "tent house") refers to our present physical body; the "house not made with hands" refers to the resurrection body that the believer expects one day. Now we groan with many sorrows and burdens (v. 4), but the day is coming in which we shall have a perfect body with which to serve God forever. We walk by faith (v. 7) and should never fear the future because our loving Savior is guiding our steps homeward. In the mean time, we are ambassadors for Christ, urging men to be reconciled to God (v. 20).

_____

Golden thought: **We have a house eternal in the heavens.**

"Wherefore we labor, that, whether present or absent, we may be accepted of him" (II Cor. 5:9).

February 5

"*F*or where two or three are gathered together in my name, there am I in the midst of them" (Matt. 18:20). The Lord Jesus has just used "this little child" as an object lesson of faith and trust in Himself (v. 4). He welcomes children and humble people in small gatherings to Himself. He is not impressed by huge assemblies in massive architecture. When just a few saints gather together in a small church or a humble prayer meeting, they may rest assured that He is present and is listening. He delights to answer the prayer of "two or three" who seek His face in humble submission. Let us take our ministry of intercessory prayer seriously, for the Lord Himself is listening.

───────────────

Golden thought: **"There am I in the midst of them."**
"God resisteth the proud, and giveth grace to the humble" (I Pet. 5:5).

February 6

A bruised reed shall he not break, and the smoking flax shall he not quench: he shall bring forth judgment unto truth" (Isa. 42:3). Isaiah prophesies of Messiah, the Servant of Jehovah, who shall deal gently with His people. Matthew quotes this verse and applies it to the Lord Jesus, in whom even the Gentiles will trust (Matt. 12:18–21). When the wick of a lamp starts smoking, most people just pull it out and quench it with water. A bruised reed cannot erect itself; most people would just uproot it and throw it away. But the Lord Jesus deals gently with broken and bruised people. He restores and transforms them into useful servants of the Lord that they might be testimonies of His grace and love.

Golden thought: **"A bruised reed shall he not break."**
The Lord has chosen the weak things of the world to confound the mighty (I Cor. 1:27).

February 7

"The Lord also will be a refuge for the oppressed, a refuge in times of trouble" (Ps. 9:9). When trouble comes, there are always some people who disappear and leave you standing alone. The Lord is not like that. He is always near when we need Him the most. A refuge is a place into which we may flee when danger comes. The Lord is always present when the emergency arises. He is our security when all else fails. The presence of the Lord gave Moses the courage he needed to face Pharaoh (Exod. 7:10). David faced Goliath with trust in God (I Sam. 17:45). We need that same serene confidence in God as our refuge whatever circumstances we may face. He alone is our protection.

Golden thought: **The Lord will be a refuge in times of trouble.**

"And they that know thy name will put their trust in thee: for thou, Lord, hast not forsaken them that seek thee" (Ps. 9:10).

February 8

"*T*here hath no temptation taken you but such as is common to man: but God is faithful, who will not suffer you to be tempted above that ye are able; but will with the temptation also make a way to escape, that ye may be able to bear it" (I Cor. 10:13). God always tempers tests by His wisdom. He knows our frailty and will not bring upon us tests greater than we can bear. There is always a right pathway that will lead us through every test. His purpose is always that we pass the test and learn how to draw upon His grace in times of need. We should forsake all trust in ourselves and depend upon His grace to bring us through (I Cor. 10:12). He will never fail His people.

Golden thought: **"God is faithful."**
"Wherefore, my dearly beloved, flee from idolatry" (I Cor. 10:14).

February 9

"*I* am the vine, ye are the branches: He that abideth in me, and I in him, the same bringeth forth much fruit: for without me ye can do nothing" (John 15:5). Just as the branch must abide in the vine to bear fruit, so the believer must abide in the Lord Jesus Christ in order to have a fruitful life. Anything that would separate the believer from Christ must be repudiated and removed in order to have unbroken fellowship and fruitfulness. The believer should be "constantly abiding," speaking to the Lord in silent prayer and thinking about His Word as he goes about his daily business. It does not mean that he neglects his work, but it does mean that he will have a sweet spirit throughout the day.

Golden thought: **Jesus said that the man who abides in Him brings forth much fruit.**

"Herein is my Father glorified, that ye bear much fruit; so shall ye be my disciples" (John 15:8).

February 10

"And he said, My presence shall go with thee, and I will give thee rest" (Exod. 33:14). God had commissioned Moses to lead His people, but Moses was struck with his own inability to do such a great thing. Here the Lord promises Moses that He will go with him and be the real power in his ministry. This same dependent relationship must be in the life of every believer. None of us can accomplish all that God desires without His enabling power. The secret of Christian service is to draw from the Word of God the strength and wisdom needed and to serve in God's power. If God is with us, we can rest in His strength and let Him use us to accomplish His purpose.

Golden thought: **"My presence shall go with thee."**

"And the Lord said unto Moses, I will do this thing also that thou hast spoken: for thou hast found grace in my sight, and I know thee by name" (Exod. 33:17).

February 11

"Heaven and earth shall pass away, but my words shall not pass away" (Matt. 24:35). The words of the Lord Jesus Christ are words of eternal life and blessing. His people will never forget them, even in eternity. There the veil will be lifted, and we shall remember them all. Now it is extremely important for believers to fill their minds and hearts with His precious words that they might strengthen their lives and testimonies. "Thy word have I hid in mine heart, that I might not sin against thee" (Ps. 119:11). The remembered Word of the Lord is a mighty resource of protection and strength. The Lord Jesus used His Word to defeat the Devil; we also may use it to break his temptations.

Golden thought: **Jesus said, "My words shall not pass away."**
Jesus said, "If ye continue in my word, then are ye my disciples indeed" (John 8:31).

February 12

"And Jesus said unto them, Come ye after me, and I will make you to become fishers of men" (Mark 1:17). The Lord Jesus called the disciples from their fishing nets so that He could transform them into fishermen for the souls of men. Believers do not "catch" people; they bring them to the Lord Jesus, and He transforms them into His saints. The humblest believer may have the privilege of bringing others to know his Lord and Savior. It is not something that believers have to strain to do. They merely allow the Lord to use them to talk about Him and tell others how much He has done for them. It is the Lord Jesus who transforms them, even as He has us.

Golden thought: **"I will make you to become fishers of men."**
Andrew "first findeth his own brother Simon, and saith unto him, We have found the Messiah" (John 1:41).

February 13

"*B*lessed are the poor in spirit: for theirs is the kingdom of heaven" (Matt. 5:3). The word *poor* does not mean "financially embarrassed"; it is the Greek word for *beggar*. The person who realizes that he is an absolute beggar before God, with no resources at all, can come to God and beg Him for forgiveness and salvation. If he comes as the Pharisee, thinking himself rich, God is not listening. But if he comes as a beggar, crying for forgiveness and salvation, God is prepared not only to forgive him but also to make him a dear child in the family of God. He will have a heavenly Father and an eternal home waiting for him in glory. He is made a child of the King.

Golden thought: **Blessed are the beggars in spirit.**

The blind beggar, Bartimaeus, cried out, "Jesus, thou Son of David, have mercy on me" (Mark 10:47).

February 14

"*B*lessed are they that mourn: for they shall be comforted" (Matt. 5:4). The person who realizes that he is lost and undone before God will grieve over his terrible condition. This is called repentance; he changes the way he is thinking. Instead of wallowing in sin, he is horrified by it. He is sorry that he has sinned against God. God is quick to forgive and comfort the penitent. His sorrow can be turned into joy, for now he is forgiven and delivered from his sin. Now he can rejoice in the salvation of God even as the Philippian jailor did (Acts 16:31–34). It is the Word of God that provides such comfort (Rom. 15:4). God is the "Father of mercies, and the God of all comfort" (II Cor. 1:3).

Golden thought: **Jesus says, "They shall be comforted."**
"Who comforts us in all our tribulation, that we may be able to comfort them which are in any trouble" (II Cor. 1:4).

February 15

"*B*lessed are the meek: for they shall inherit the earth" (Matt. 5:5). The meek are those who are humble, gentle, and considerate of others. They are a contrast to proud landowners, business magnates, and political authorities who are used to ordering people about. The meek walk humbly with God, seeking to do His will. The Lord Jesus Himself claimed to be "meek and lowly" (Matt. 11:29). He always did those things that pleased His Father (John 8:29). He was not weak but always pleasing to His Father. The meek shall inherit the earth, but beyond that they shall inherit the courts of heaven as well. They have sorrow and crying in this life but will inherit all things in glory (Rev. 21:4–7).

Golden thought: **The meek shall inherit the earth.**

"The Lord lifteth up the meek: he casteth the wicked down to the ground" (Ps. 147:6).

February 16

"*B*lessed are they which do hunger and thirst after righteousness: for they shall be filled" (Matt. 5:6). Apart from the Lord Jesus Christ "there is none righteous, no not one" (Rom. 3:10); the righteousness of God comes by faith in Jesus Christ (Rom. 3:22); the righteousness of Christ is imputed to the believer (Rom. 4:11); there is no condemnation to them which are in Christ Jesus (Rom. 8:1); now the believer should present his body a living sacrifice to God (Rom. 12:1). The day will come when God shall dwell with His righteous people in a new heaven and new earth (Rev. 21:3). Now our hearts should long for that perfect righteousness. _____

Golden thought: **They shall be filled with righteousness.**
His name shall be called "THE LORD OUR RIGHTEOUSNESS" (Jer. 23:6).

February 17

"*B*lessed are the merciful: for they shall obtain mercy" (Matt. 5:7). When a person receives the mercy and grace of God in Christ, it is a life-transforming experience. God is rich in mercy (Eph. 2:4). According to His mercy He saved us (Titus 3:5). God is "the Father of mercies" (II Cor. 1:3). When a person has received such mercy from God, it is fitting for him to show to others. James warns, "For he shall have judgment without mercy, that hath shewed no mercy; and mercy rejoiceth against judgment" (2:13). A person who has received the mercy of God in Christ will manifest a merciful spirit toward others.

Golden thought: **"They shall obtain mercy."**
"The Lord is very pitiful, and of tender mercy" (James 5:11).

February 18

"*B*lessed are the pure in heart: for they shall see God" (Matt. 5:8). When Moses saw the burning bush, he knew it was a divine vision and was afraid to look at it (Exod. 3:6). The sight of absolute holiness would consume a sinful man. But the grace of Christ purifies the heart and life of the believer. The day will come when we shall see Him face to face and not be consumed. We shall be changed into the same image (II Cor. 3:18), an image of true holiness. The promise to the saints in glory is "And they shall see his face; and his name shall be in their foreheads" (Rev. 22:4). They will bear the character of Christ and shall see God face to face.

Golden thought: "**They shall see God.**"
"The city had no need of the sun, neither of the moon, to shine in it: for the glory of God did lighten it, and the Lamb is the light thereof" (Rev. 21:23).

February 19

"*B*lessed are the peacemakers: for they shall be called the children of God" (Matt. 5:9). When the believer has made his peace with God and has been reconciled to God through the Lord Jesus Christ, he is now a person devoted to peace. The world is sunk in wars. There are military wars, social wars, class wars, religious wars, and personal vendettas. But the believer, now at peace with God, wishes also to be at peace with his neighbor. He is a peacemaker to all because he knows that God is the answer to all wars and conflicts. The first step is getting right with God, peace with God, and then seeking peace with others to the glory of God.

Golden thought: **Peacemakers shall be called the children of God.**
"Now the God of peace be with you all. Amen" (Rom. 15:33).

February 20

"*B*lessed are they which are persecuted for righteousness' sake: for theirs is the kingdom of heaven" (Matt. 5:10). No one relishes the thought of being persecuted, but when the persecution comes because of being on God's side, it is a different matter. The Lord Jesus Christ, the Prince of peace, was persecuted by the religious leaders of His day. He was murdered by governmental authorities. Yet His prayer was "Father, forgive them; for they know not what they do" (Luke 23:34). The believer in Christ should count any persecution that he encounters the highest privilege that he can receive. To suffer for the sake of Christ should cause joy, not sorrow.

Golden thought: **The kingdom of heaven belongs to the persecuted.**

"Love . . . endureth all things" (I Cor. 13:7).

February 21

"*B*lessed are ye, when men shall revile you, and persecute you, and shall say all manner of evil against you falsely, for my sake. Rejoice, and be exceeding glad: for great is your reward in heaven: for so persecuted they the prophets which were before you" (Matt. 5:11–12). This is a personal application. What if the persecution should actually come to me? It would be a glorious opportunity to stand in the company of the great prophets of old. Evil men reviled and slandered God's servants in the past. It would be a great honor for us to bear reproach for the sake of Christ. God has already planned celebration in heaven for those who endure persecution for the sake of His Son.

Golden thought: **Blessed are you when men shall revile you for Christ's sake.**

"Ye are the salt of the earth . . . ye are the light of the world" (Matt. 5:13–14).

February 22

"*He* hath said, I will never leave thee, nor forsake thee. So that we may boldly say, The Lord is my helper, and I will not fear what man shall do unto me" (Heb. 13:5–6). God gave this promise to Joshua to encourage him to conquer the Promised Land (Deut. 31:6). The writer of Hebrews extends this promise to all who may live in danger for the sake of the Lord. If the Lord is our Helper, there are no grounds for fear. God is able to protect us. Thus, the believer should be neither reckless nor fearful. We should do our work for Him with the serene confidence that our Lord is unchangeable. He has always kept His promises and will always keep them to us as well.

Golden thought: **God says, "I will never leave thee, nor forsake thee."**

"Jesus Christ the same yesterday, and to day, and for ever" (Heb. 13:8).

February 23

"*F*or thou wilt light my candle: the Lord my God will enlighten my darkness" (Ps. 18:28). David had many occasions when the darkness oppressed him, but he always looked to the Lord to rescue him. He called upon the Lord for deliverance, and the Lord delivered him (Ps. 18:3). He confessed that "the floods of ungodly men made me afraid" (v. 4). But he called upon the Lord, and He heard him (v. 6). Believers should take courage from David's example. God is always ready to hear the prayers of His people. Whatever darkness we may be in, the Lord is always able to shine the light of His presence into our hearts and illuminate our pathway by His Word.

Golden thought: **God will enlighten my darkness.**

"The Lord is my rock, and my fortress, and my deliverer; my God, my strength" (Ps. 18:2).

February 24

"*A*nd the Lord shall guide thee continually, and satisfy thy soul in drought" (Isa. 58:11). Isaiah called upon his people to forsake their sins and call upon Jehovah God (vv. 1, 9). The Lord was able to guide them, but they would not follow His leading. We must remember to turn away from all that displeases the Lord and to obey the clear teaching of His Word. The Lord is able to guide us through His Word just as surely as He guided the Israelites. Even in drought the Lord can sustain His people. When believers obey God, He promises, "Thou shalt be like a watered garden" (v. 11). A spring of refreshing water flows into the heart of every obedient believer.

Golden thought: **The Lord shall guide you continually.**

"Then thou shalt call, and the Lord shall answer; thou shalt cry, and he shall say, Here am I" (Isa. 58:9).

February 25

"*T*he Lord is my shepherd; I shall not want" (Ps. 23:1). David's experience as a shepherd gave him great understanding of God's care for His people. David would never have abandoned a single sheep. How much more certain that God will never abandon His sheep! The Lord will lead His sheep to the green pastures and the still waters that they need. The Lord will lead His people through the darkest valleys in safety. David was certain that goodness and mercy would follow him all his days. But he clearly expresses his faith in the eternal life that God provides for His people. "I will dwell in the house of the Lord forever" (v. 6).

Golden thought: **"The Lord is my shepherd."**

"I am the good shepherd, and know my sheep, and am known of mine" (John 10:14).

February 26

"*M*y sheep hear my voice, and I know them, and they follow me: and I give unto them eternal life; and they shall never perish, neither shall any man pluck them out of my hand" (John 10:27–28). The Lord Jesus clearly removes all doubt about continued life beyond the grave for His people. He promises them eternal life and assures them that no one is able to take them out of His care. The believer who humbly follows the Lord Jesus here will continue following Him throughout eternity. He promises that they will never perish because He will hold them in the hollow of His hand. We may safely trust in the keeping power of the great Shepherd of the sheep.

Golden thought: **Jesus says, "I give unto them eternal life, and they shall never perish."**

You "are now returned unto the Shepherd and Bishop of your souls" (I Pet. 2:25).

February 27

"*I* will fear no evil: for thou art with me; thy rod and thy staff they comfort me" (Ps. 23:4). The picture of the sheep calmly feeding while the shepherd watches is a beautiful portrait of Christ's constant care for His people. The rod was a sturdy club that the shepherd would use to fight off any wolf or jackal that might appear. The staff was a pole, often with a crook at the top, that the shepherd could use to guide the sheep, or even to rescue them from a crevice they might fall into. The mere presence of the shepherd was the promise of protection and care to every sheep. The believer can rest in the protection of the Good Shepherd.

Golden thought: **"Thou art with me."**

"Surely the righteous shall give thanks unto thy name: the upright shall dwell in thy presence" (Ps. 140:13).

February 28

"*K*now ye that the Lord he is God: it is he that hath made us, and not we ourselves; we are his people, and the sheep of his pasture" (Ps. 100:3). There is a promise in the fact that believers are God's people, the sheep He cares for. We ought to be a joyful people. "Serve the Lord with gladness: come before his presence with singing" (v. 2). As God's sheep we ought to be thankful for every mouthful of sweet clover that He provides for us. We must not take His care for us for granted. The Good Shepherd is always true to His nature. "For the Lord is good; his mercy is everlasting; and his truth endureth to all generations" (v. 5).

Golden thought: **"We are his people, and the sheep of his pasture."**
"Let us come before his presence with thanksgiving, and make a joyful noise unto him with psalms" (Ps. 95:2).

February 29

"*I* returned, and saw under the sun, that the race is not to the swift, nor the battle to the strong, . . . but time and chance happeneth to them all" (Eccles. 9:11). God is the only being who can control time and chance. David expressed it well, "My times are in thy hand" (Ps. 31:15). The Lord Jesus Christ holds the keys of hades and death (Rev. 1:18). Concerning chance, Solomon had it right: "The lot is cast into the lap; but the whole disposing thereof is of the Lord" (Prov. 16:33). That is why David prayed, "In thee, O Lord, do I put my trust" (Ps. 31:1). "Be thou my strong rock" (Ps. 31:2). "Make thy face to shine upon thy servant: save me for thy mercies' sake" (Ps. 31:16).

Golden thought: **My times are in His hand.**
"Be of good courage, and he shall strengthen your heart, all ye that hope in the Lord" (Ps. 31:24).

March 1

*J*esus said, "He that heareth my word, and believeth on him that sent me, hath everlasting life, and shall not come into condemnation; but is passed from death unto life" (John 5:24). Trust in the Lord Jesus as Savior frees one from the guilt of the past and future condemnation. All men should honor the Son even as they honor the Father (John 5:23), for the Father has committed all judgment unto the Son (v. 22). Paul warns, "For the wages of sin is death; but the gift of God is eternal life through Jesus Christ our Lord" (Rom. 6:23). Jesus is "the Lamb of God, which taketh away the sin of the world" (John 1:29). If you do not know Him as Savior, ask Him now to blot out your sins and make you His child.

——————————————————

Golden thought: **He who hears and believes on Jesus has everlasting life.**

Jesus said, "Search the Scriptures; for in them ye think ye have eternal life: and they are they which testify of me" (John 5:39).

March 2

"And Jesus said unto them, I am the bread of life: he that cometh to me shall never hunger; and he that believeth on me shall never thirst" (John 6:35). The Lord Jesus satisfies perfectly. He is the living bread that feeds the souls of those who trust in Him (John 6:51). In the ancient world bread was the staff of life. It was brown bread, filled with nutrition. The Lord uses this illustration to teach us the sustaining power of His grace. If He is your Savior, you will never have that desolate feeling of emptiness within. He dwells in the heart of every believer. His grace sustains and strengthens each believer that he might accomplish God's will every day.

Golden thought: **Jesus said, "I am the bread of life."**
"This is the bread which cometh down from heaven, that a man may eat thereof, and not die" (John 6:50).

March 3

*J*esus said, "If any man thirst, let him come unto me, and drink" (John 7:37). We sometimes walk though "a dry and thirsty land, where no water is" (Ps. 63:1). But when our souls thirst for God, we may come to the Lord Jesus to find the water of life that sustains our souls. The believer who meditates in the word of the Lord "shall be like a tree planted by the rivers of water, that bringeth forth his fruit in his season; his leaf also shall not wither" (Ps. 1:3). The grace of the Lord Jesus refreshes the soul and strengthens the life of the believer. Without Him, we walk through a spiritual desert with no hope, but with Him we walk in refreshment and fellowship with the Lord of all.

Golden thought: **Jesus said, "Come unto me, and drink."**
"As the hart panteth after the water brooks, so panteth my soul after thee, O God" (Ps. 42:1).

March 4

"Now therefore go, and I will be with thy mouth, and teach thee what thou shalt say" (Exod. 4:12). The Lord spoke these words to Moses, commanding him to go to Pharaoh to ask for the release of His people. Moses had complained that he was not an eloquent speaker (Exod. 4:10). But that does not matter, for the message was the Lord's. All Moses had to do was to repeat it. Believers today are still troubled by the same timidity. But no one is ever saved by the eloquence of the witness. A person is saved only by the grace of God. We can all claim this precious promise and give our humble testimony for Christ. Only God can cause the seed of the Word to take root in the heart and bring forth fruit.

Golden thought: **"I will be with thy mouth."**
"Then Philip opened his mouth, and began at the same scripture, and preached unto him Jesus" (Acts 8:35).

March 5

"*B*lessed is that man that maketh the Lord his trust, and respecteth not the proud, nor such as turn aside to lies" (Ps. 40:4). The man who trusts in the Lord is happy, divinely gifted with joy, because God Himself blesses such trust. God is not burdened or troubled by people who call upon Him for help. He is fully able to hear and answer their cries. David exclaimed that God had brought him up out of a horrible pit "and set my feet upon a rock" (v. 2). God is able to rescue every saint who calls upon Him. But those who are proud and think they do not need God's help, or turn aside to the lies of human sufficiency, are on the slippery slope to the miry clay.

Golden thought: **Blessed is the man who trusts in the Lord.**
"In God I have put my trust; I will not fear what flesh can do unto me" (Ps. 56:4).

March 6

"*T*he Lord is nigh unto all them that call upon him, to all that call upon him in truth" (Ps. 145:18). The Lord is not a God who is far off. When the believer needs divine help, God is very near. Although some people just make a show of praying to God, their heart is far removed from Him. But for those who truly ask the Lord for help, God is an ever-present source of help. He hears their cries, but beyond that He knows exactly what kind of help to provide for them. Sometimes believers ask unwisely, but God always knows the perfect answer to their prayers. Believers should never tell God how to answer their prayers. They should always trust Him to provide the right answer with the right means.

Golden thought: **The Lord is near to all who call upon Him.**

"I will call upon the Lord, who is worthy to be praised: so shall I be saved from mine enemies" (Ps. 18:3).

March 7

"*B*e careful for nothing; but in every thing by prayer and supplication with thanksgiving let your requests be made known unto God. And the peace of God, which passeth all understanding, shall keep your hearts and minds through Christ Jesus" (Phil. 4:6–7). Believers must not be worriers. When we come to God with our requests, we must recognize His love, power, and wisdom. We can safely lay our burdens at His feet, knowing that His answer will be perfect. The peace of God will guard our hearts like a garrison guarding a city. All God's answers come through Jesus Christ. He is our Intercessor, our Savior. He can provide for all our needs by His grace.

Golden thought: **The peace of God shall guard our hearts.**

"If there be any praise, think on these things" (Phil. 4:8).

March 8

"Now unto him that is able to keep you from falling, and to present you faultless before the presence of his glory with exceeding joy, to the only wise God our Saviour, be glory and majesty, dominion and power, both now and ever. Amen" (Jude 24–25). Although the believer may have doubts about his own ability to keep from falling, he should have no doubt at all about the Lord's ability. We walk by faith and should have serene trust in the Lord's keeping power. He can give us the grace and spiritual strength we need. His purpose is not just to preserve us today but to carry us all the way through to glory in His presence. We must trust Him every step of the way.

Golden thought: **God our Savior is able to keep you from falling.** "Holy Father, keep through thine own name those whom thou hast given me" (John 17:11).

March 9

"*B*lessed is the man that trusteth in the Lord, and whose hope the Lord is. For he shall be as a tree planted by the waters, and that spreadeth out her roots by the river, and shall not see when heat cometh, but her leaf shall be green" (Jer. 17:7–8). Trust in the Lord strengthens the character of the believer. He becomes like the tree that has roots that run underground to a stream. There is a constant supply of strength and energy pouring into the tree and into the believer! Such a tree regularly bears fruit. The believer also should draw upon the strength of the Lord and constantly bear fruit to the glory of God. Trust in God draws hidden strength to every believer.

Golden thought: **"He shall be as a tree planted by the waters."**
"I laid me down and slept; I awaked; for the Lord sustained me" (Ps. 3:5).

March 10

"*I*n the day of my trouble I will call upon thee: for thou wilt answer me" (Ps. 86:7). When trouble comes, the arm of flesh will fail us. We dare not trust ourselves. But David turned to God and called upon Him. We should also turn to God first. The gods of the heathen cannot help them, for they are merely idols. But we serve the living God and should be quick to turn to Him in times of trouble. David was sure that God would answer him. We ought to have a similar trust in the living God. When any trouble comes, we should never worry or fret. We should spread our plight before God and ask Him to be our strength and comfort. God is "full of compassion, and gracious, longsuffering, and plenteous in mercy and truth" (Ps. 86:15).

Golden thought: **God will answer me.**

"O turn unto me, and have mercy upon me" (Ps. 86:16).

March 11

"Come now, and let us reason together, saith the Lord: though your sins be as scarlet, they shall be as white as snow; though they be red like crimson, they shall be as wool" (Isa. 1:18). God invites people to come to Him that He might blot out their sins. People try to gloss over their sins, or merely to hide them, but God knows the heart of every person. God alone can remove sin through the cleansing power of the blood of His dear Son, the Lord Jesus Christ. "God for Christ's sake hath forgiven you" (Eph. 4:32). There is no reason for the sinner to perish when Christ will extend forgiveness to him. But the sinner needs to come to the Lord Jesus to ask Him to blot out his sins and iniquities.

Golden thought: **"Though your sins be as scarlet, they shall be as white as snow."**

"For thou, Lord, art good, and ready to forgive; and plenteous in mercy unto all them that call upon thee" (Ps. 86:5).

March 12

"*C*ome unto me, all ye that labour and are heavy laden, and I will give you rest" (Matt. 11:28). The Lord Jesus Christ here gives a universal invitation because all of sinful mankind labors and struggles with lack of rest. The trouble is that people are trying to accomplish their own purposes, to amass their own wealth or influence, instead of submitting to God. Those who come to Christ will find that He can lift their burdens and give them new direction in God's will. By the grace of Christ, it is possible to serve God, and the burden is much lighter. His rest is rest from selfishness and greed. It means the service of God with joy and peace and blessing toward others.

Golden thought: **"I will give you rest."**
Jesus says, "For my yoke is easy, and my burden is light" (Matt. 11:30).

March 13

"The effectual fervent prayer of a righteous man availeth much" (James 5:16). Literally, the Greek text reads, "An effective prayer of a righteous man is strong for much." The Bible lays great stress on the power of prayer. God is listening. He is prepared to work mightily in behalf of His saints. Souls are saved because people pray. Churches grow stronger because saints pray. God blesses the ministry of pastors, soulwinners, and missionaries because people pray. James goes on to mention the ministry of Elijah. He was a normal human being, but he worked miracles through prayer. Believers today ought to pray fervently that God will work powerfully in our day to accomplish His great work through us.

Golden thought: **Prayer avails much.**

"Pray without ceasing" (I Thess. 5:17).

March 14

"For whosoever shall call upon the name of the Lord shall be saved" (Rom. 10:13; Acts 2:21). This is a promise so important that it is given twice in the New Testament and once in the Old (Joel 2:32). God wants all people to know that it is unimportant who they are. What is important is that they call upon Him for salvation. God is no respecter of persons. He hears the cry of every human being who will beg for forgiveness and cleansing from sin through His Son, Jesus Christ. Being saved does not mean merely avoiding hell; it means becoming a child of God, a servant of Jesus Christ. Now the believer can tell others about the greatness of the love of God that saves to the uttermost those who call upon Him.

_____

Golden thought: **Whoever calls upon the Lord shall be saved.**
"I have called upon thee, for thou wilt hear me, O God" (Ps. 17:6).

March 15

"*I*f thou shalt confess with thy mouth the Lord Jesus, and shalt believe in thine heart that God hath raised him from the dead, thou shalt be saved" (Rom. 10:9). The death of Jesus Christ was not that of a martyr; it was that of the Son of God who gave Himself for the sins of the world. Salvation is not merely head knowledge; it is heart surrender to the Lord that He might forgive, transform, and empower the believer to a new life of service for God. Now the believer can live for God; he can find a group of believers and identify himself with the people of God, the church that Jesus Christ died to save. The believer should now seek out a Bible-believing church and worship Christ publicly.

Golden thought: **If you confess the Lord Jesus, you shall be saved.**
"For with the heart man believeth unto righteousness; and with the mouth confession is made unto salvation" (Rom. 10:10).

March 16

"*F*or I am not ashamed of the gospel of Christ: for it is the power of God unto salvation . . . to the Jew first, and also to the Greek" (Rom. 1:16). That Christ died for the sins of the world is the great evangel that brings salvation to believers whatever their nation or race. The Jews had the Old Testament Scriptures, but now the completed Bible heralds forth God's salvation to all the world. Whosoever will may come to Christ. This is why the Bible is translated into hundreds of languages, that every nation and language may have the record of Christ's dying for the sins of the world. Whosoever will may come and be saved by the blood of the Lamb of God.

———————————————

Golden thought: **The gospel of Christ is the power of God unto salvation.**

"There is therefore now no condemnation to them which are in Christ Jesus, who walk not after the flesh, but after the Spirit" (Rom. 8:1).

March 17

"*B*ut to him that worketh not, but believeth on him that justifieth the ungodly, his faith is counted for righteousness" (Rom. 4:5). Christianity is not a "works" religion; it is a religion of faith and trust in Christ. No one can do enough to atone for his sins and be saved. The Lord Jesus Christ, by His death for our sins, can cleanse away every stain and make us pure before God. God accepts the faith of the believer in Christ and credits the righteousness of Christ to the believer. "Blessed is the man to whom the Lord will not impute sin" (Rom. 4:8). Instead God imputes the righteousness of Christ: "But for us also, to whom it shall be imputed, if we believe on him that raised up Jesus our Lord from the dead" (Rom. 4:24).

_____

Golden thought: **"His faith is counted for righteousness."**
"But God commendeth his love toward us, in that, while we were yet sinners, Christ died for us" (Rom. 5:8).

March 18

"*Thou* shalt guide me with thy counsel, and afterward receive me to glory" (Ps. 73:24). The psalmist expresses his sincere faith in God. Although his steps had almost slipped (v. 2), and he had endured plagues and chastening (v. 14), he was confident that God would give him the guidance he needed. He was sure that God was constantly with him and was leading him by his right hand (v. 23). When he came to the end of his earthly life, he expected God to receive him into His presence. He asks, "Whom have I in heaven but thee?" (v. 25). There was none to plead his cause but God Himself. He concludes, "But it is good for me to draw near to God: I have put my trust in the Lord God, that I may declare all thy works" (v. 28).

Golden thought: **You will guide me and receive me to glory.**
"I will remember the works of the Lord" (Ps. 77:11).

March 19

"*F*or I know the thoughts that I think toward you, saith the Lord, thoughts of peace, and not of evil, to give you an expected end" (Jer. 29:11). God's intention toward His people is always help and ultimate blessing. But there are times when He must bring chastisement upon them. He had brought seventy years of captivity upon Israel because of their sins (Jer. 29:10), but that was intended to bring them back to Himself. So He brings trials upon believers, but never to harm them, only to cause them to return to Him. The end that we may expect of the Lord is gracious restoration and blessing. We should look with the eyes of faith upon all trials and expect the Lord to bring about blessing through them all.

Golden thought: **The Lord has thoughts of peace toward His people.**

"Then shall ye call upon me, and ye shall go and pray unto me, and I will hearken unto you" (Jer. 29:12).

March 20

"*A*nd ye shall seek me, and find me, when ye shall search for me with all your heart" (Jer. 29:13). Every believer needs a single-minded devotion for the Lord. Having a divided mind is a sure way of losing fellowship with the Lord. But when we delight in the Lord and seek Him eagerly, He becomes very precious to us and the fires of devotion burn within us. Searching the Scriptures can cause our hearts to draw near the Lord and rejoice in His loving care. We need to fill our minds with the Word of God that He may rekindle the fires of love toward Him that we need. "Thou hast been my help; leave me not, neither forsake me, O God of my salvation" (Ps. 27:9).

―――――――――――――――――――

Golden thought: **"Ye shall seek me, and find me."**
"Teach me thy way, O Lord, and lead me in a plain path" (Ps. 27:11).

March 21

"*W*ait on the Lord: be of good courage, and he shall strengthen thine heart: wait, I say, on the Lord" (Ps. 27:14). It is always hard to wait, but the Lord is not in a hurry. We need to learn that fellowship with the Lord is more important than securing that petition we have. As we wait on Him, He conforms us to His purpose and strengthens us to accomplish His will. Time spent with Him is more precious than gold. Thinking about the Lord always calms us and helps us have the right perspective on life. The psalmist repeats the command to wait because it is so important for us to spend time in the presence of God. We should not wait on the Lord only when we need something.

Golden thought: **Wait on the Lord, and He shall strengthen your heart.**

"The Lord is my light and my salvation; whom shall I fear?" (Ps. 27:1).

March 22

"*H*umble yourselves in the sight of the Lord, and he shall lift you up" (James 4:10). When believers act in pride, they get into trouble. Solomon warns, "Pride goeth before destruction, and an haughty spirit before a fall" (Prov. 16:18). We can honestly confess that we are poor, unprofitable servants who have nothing to boast about. Every time we begin to think we are somebody, the Lord deflates us. We need to learn to walk humbly with God. He is the one who is great and exalted. We should give all honor and glory to Him. If God honors us, we can continue our humble walk with Him and give Him all the glory. We owe everything we are, and everything we have, to Him.

Golden thought: **"He shall lift you up."**

"Rejoice in the Lord alway: and again I say, Rejoice" (Phil. 4:4).

March 23

"When a man's ways please the Lord, he maketh even his enemies to be at peace with him" (Prov. 16:7). Pleasing the Lord should have first place in the believer's life. Whenever the believer puts the Lord first, He can rearrange things so that they move in a better direction. Enemies can be implacable, but if the Lord touches their heart, they can change. We should concentrate on pleasing the Lord and leave to Him the trials and problems that surround us. In time, the Lord may even convert foes to become brothers in the Lord. Paul did not try to please men but God (I Thess. 2:4). Our burden should be to walk worthy of the Lord (I Thess. 2:12).

_____

Golden thought: **Please the Lord and even enemies can be at peace.**

"And whatsoever we ask, we receive of him, because we keep his commandments, and do those things that are pleasing in his sight" (I John 3:22).

March 24

"*B*ut seek ye first the kingdom of God, and his righteousness; and all these things shall be added unto you" (Matt. 6:33). People in the world center their thoughts on the food, possessions, and luxuries that they wish to enjoy. The Lord shows us that these are minor details. The really important things in life center in the will and purpose of God. That we might have His righteousness is vastly more important than any quantity of "things." We need to seek His face for the righteousness that is found in Jesus Christ alone. He died upon the cross that we might have His righteousness as a free gift to all who trust Him as Savior. The treasures of this world soon pass away, but salvation in Christ is forever.

———————————————————

Golden thought: **Seek God first and all necessary things will follow.**

The Macedonian churches "first gave their own selves to the Lord" (II Cor. 8:5).

March 25

"Ye shall not fear them: for the Lord your God he shall fight for you" (Deut. 3:22). The Israelites were not to fear the strong nations that were before them. The children of Israel were slow to realize what that meant, but in time they saw the Lord defeat one nation after another until the land was theirs. Believers today often fear enemies and situations that lie before them. They should remember how great the Lord is. He can defeat our foes and bring us to victory in any situation we face. But we must trust Him and walk in humble obedience to His commands. The victory will come in His own good time. Trust Him and obey His Word.

Golden thought: **The Lord your God shall fight for you.**
"Fight the good fight of faith, lay hold on eternal life" (I Tim. 6:12).

March 26

"*B*ut if from thence thou shalt seek the Lord thy God, thou shalt find him, if thou seek him with all thy heart and with all thy soul" (Deut. 4:29). Half-hearted worship is an insult to the Lord. He is Lord of heaven and earth and deserves the best that is within us. If we seek Him with all our heart, He promises that we shall find Him. That should stir us up to search the Scriptures to see more of His revelation of Himself in His Word. As we meditate on the blessed portrait of God in His Word, we will find ourselves moved to greater obedience and service. With that comes a greater perception of His divine nature, love, and majesty. But God is infinitely greater than our best perception. Keep seeking Him.

Golden thought: **If you seek the Lord your God, you will find Him.**

"If ye then be risen with Christ, seek those things which are above, where Christ sitteth on the right hand of God" (Col. 3:1).

March 27

"*T*his book of the law shall not depart out of thy mouth; but thou shalt meditate therein day and night, that thou mayest observe to do according to all that is written therein: for then thou shalt make thy way prosperous, and then thou shalt have good success" (Josh. 1:8). Meditating on Scripture was the secret of Joshua's success. He was not intimidated by the armies he had to face or the fortified cities he had to conquer. Day and night he was thinking about the Word of God and the promises God had given him. Every believer should be thinking about the greatness of God and the clear promises of help in Scripture. God is great enough to overcome all the foes we face if we just meditate on His Word.

Golden thought: **Meditate on the Word; then you shall have good success.**

"All scripture is given by inspiration of God, and is profitable for doctrine, for reproof, for correction, for instruction in righteousness" (II Tim. 3:16).

March 28

"*H*ave not I commanded thee? Be strong and of good courage; be not afraid, neither be thou dismayed: for the Lord thy God is with thee whithersoever thou goest" (Josh. 1:9). The Lord strengthens and reassures Joshua for the conquest of the land. Every believer needs to recognize that God is with him as he faces the trials and adversaries of the Christian life. He never has to face the foe alone. Just as the Lord was with Joshua through the conquest of the land, so He will be with the believer today throughout the Christian life. The presence of God with the believer is the great secret of success in the Christian life. Fear has no place in the heart of the believer. God is all-sufficient.

Golden thought: **Be strong and of good courage . . . the Lord thy God is with thee.**

"When the wicked, even mine enemies and my foes, came upon me to eat up my flesh, they stumbled and fell" (Ps. 27:2).

March 29

"But thanks be to God, which giveth us the victory through our Lord Jesus Christ" (I Cor. 15:57). The believer ought to be profoundly thankful he does not have to win the battles of the Christian life by his own strength. God graciously gives His people the victory through the sacrifice of His dear Son, the Lord Jesus Christ. We not only have victory over sin in this life; we also have victory over death and the grave in the next life. The resurrection of Christ is the guarantee that He shall raise up His people at the last day. "Therefore, my beloved brethren, be ye stedfast, unmoveable, always abounding in the work of the Lord, forasmuch as ye know that your labor is not in vain in the Lord" (v. 58).

Golden thought: **God gives us the victory through our Lord Jesus Christ.**

"For the kingdom of God is not in word, but in power" (I Cor. 4:20).

March 30

"And God is able to make all grace abound toward you; that ye, always having all sufficiency in all things, may abound to every good work" (II Cor. 9:8). The Lord does not wish to impart just a bare minimum of grace to His people; He wishes to pour out all grace upon them. His purpose is that His people may have all the grace they need for every good work of service He may call them to. We should boldly ask the Lord to give us grace for every act of service we must perform. His grace is the only thing that will make our service effective. Self effort is hopeless. But the grace of God can transform us into effective witnesses for the Lord Jesus Christ.

Golden thought: **"God is able to make all grace abound toward you."**

"But he that glorieth, let him glory in the Lord" (II Cor. 10:17).

March 31

"*B*e perfect, be of good comfort, be of one mind, live in peace; and the God of love and peace shall be with you" (II Cor. 13:11). The command "be perfect" literally means "be well equipped." Believers should allow the Spirit of God to equip them for service, to comfort them and give them unity and peace. Then they can serve God effectively by His grace. The God of love and peace shall be with His faithful servants. His presence shall uphold and strengthen them to the work that He directs them to fulfill. We must never make the mistake of trying to serve God in our own strength and wisdom. He alone can give us a ministry with results that will last for all eternity.

Golden thought: **The God of love and peace shall be with you.**

"The grace of the Lord Jesus Christ . . . be with you all" (II Cor. 13:14).

April 1

"The law of the Lord is perfect, converting the soul" (Ps. 19:7). The Bible is God's perfect revelation to the heart of sinful man. Man can find no rest or peace in his soul until he gets right with God. But when a person believes the Bible and turns to God, trusting His promises, his soul is saved by the grace of the Lord Jesus. No one can save himself, but the Bible can change the heart and transform the life by the power of God. That is the reason that believers should be searching the Scriptures and meditating upon them. They need their life turned about to a new direction: toward God. The study of the Bible provides that grace and strength every believer needs to be a faithful servant for the Lord.

Golden thought: **The law of the Lord converts the soul.**
"Turn us, O God of our salvation" (Ps. 85:4).

April 2

"*In* returning and rest shall ye be saved; in quietness and in confidence shall be your strength" (Isa. 30:15). The Lord God is the protector of His people. When they rest on His promises, they are most secure. Believers do not have to scramble about, frantically struggling, to accomplish God's will. Confidence in the power and strength of God is the proper response of the saints in all trials. Israel had trusted in their horses, but they should have trusted in their God (v. 16). God has respect for those who have quiet confidence in His Word. When we walk in faith in His Word, He will order our steps according to His perfect will. If the Lord of the universe is for us, who can be against us?

Golden thought: **Confidence in God is our strength.**

"In the fear of the Lord is strong confidence: and his children shall have a place of refuge" (Prov. 14:26).

April 3

"Cast thy burden upon the Lord, and he shall sustain thee: he shall never suffer the righteous to be moved" (Ps. 55:22). All of God's people have burdens of some kind. We must learn the spiritual secret of casting those burdens on the Lord, letting Him carry the stressful items we tend to fret over. He will never allow trials and burdens to harm His people. We must ask Him for grace and strength in time of need. Putting our burdens into the Lord's hand is a sure way of finding relief from worry and stress. He will not allow "things" to harm His people. If He is carrying our burden, we will not feel the crushing load, whatever the trial is. His sustaining grace is sufficient for every burden we have.

Golden thought: **He shall sustain you.**
"I laid me down and slept; I awaked; for the Lord sustained me" (Ps. 3:5).

April 4

"*H*e that doeth the will of God abideth for ever" (I John 2:17). God's Word warns us against fascination with what is in the world. "Love not the world, neither the things that are in the world" (I John 2:15). The world is in the process of passing away. One day it will be gone forever. God's people should set their hearts on things above, where Christ sits on the right hand of God (Col. 3:1–2). We must deliberately consecrate ourselves to doing the will of God. The direction of our life must be toward Him. The world will perish, but God's people will abide forever in His presence. We must not love the world because it is passing away. God cannot pass away, and His people are secure in Him.

Golden thought: **He that does the will of God abides forever.**
"Epaphras . . . is . . . always labouring fervently for you in prayers, that ye may stand perfect and complete in all the will of God" (Col. 4:12).

April 5

"*H*e is the Rock, his work is perfect: for all his ways are judgment: a God of truth and without iniquity, just and right is he" (Deut. 32:4). The very nature of God is a promise that His people should take seriously. God is absolutely perfect, unchangeable, and just in all His deeds. He is a God of truth and would never mislead His people. His revelation in His Word is sure and without error. Just and right is He in all His dealings with mankind. We may trust Him to keep His promises perfectly. Our confidence should never be in ourselves; it should always be in the Lord God, who has given to us precious promises in His Word that He will surely keep. "Ascribe ye greatness unto our God" (Deut. 32:3).

Golden thought: **He is a God of truth; just and right is He.**

"My soul cleaveth unto the dust: quicken thou me according to thy word" (Ps. 119:25).

April 6

"For the Lord God is a sun and shield: the Lord will give grace and glory: no good thing will he withhold from them that walk uprightly" (Ps. 84:11). The psalmist uses poetic imagery to portray how great God's love is to the believer. He is like the sun shining upon the believer with grace and glory for him. He will never withhold anything that is for the believer's benefit. God delights in providing grace day after day to sustain and strengthen His child. We have a solemn responsibility to walk uprightly before Him because He is guiding our steps with loving care. His presence is a shield of protection from all harm. Our hearts should rejoice in the presence of such a loving God.

Golden thought: **The Lord God is a sun and a shield.**

"O Lord of hosts, blessed is the man who trusteth in thee" (Ps. 84:12).

April 7

"O my dove, that art in the clefts of the rock, in the secret places of the stairs, let me see thy countenance, let me hear thy voice; for sweet is thy voice, and thy countenance is comely" (Song of Sol. 2:14). The royal bridegroom speaks to his bride and invites her to come and fellowship with him. This imagery portrays the love of God for His people. God invites us to come into His presence and have sweet fellowship with Him. Day by day our prayer life with God is of vital importance to us. How can we keep the heavenly Bridegroom waiting while we attend to lesser tasks? Our hearts should leap at the thought of having sweet fellowship with God, who promises to listen and pour out His love upon us.

Golden thought: **God says, "Let me hear thy voice; for sweet is thy voice."**

"My beloved is mine, and I am his" (Song of Sol. 2:16).

April 8

"*B*lessed is the man that endureth temptation: for when he is tried, he shall receive the crown of life, which the Lord hath promised to them that love him" (James 1:12). The Lord not only saves people but also promises them crowns as well. How gracious is our loving God. His only request is that we love Him in return. Believers tend to think that temptation is a terrible ordeal, but it is really a steppingstone to greater love and fellowship with God, who sustains us. God never brings temptation upon us to harm us but to cause us to draw closer to Him and to seek more grace from His loving protection. How blessed we are to have a God who is waiting to give us the crown of life in His love.

Golden thought: **The Lord has promised the crown of life to those who love Him.**

"But be ye doers of the word, and not hearers only" (James 1:22).

April 9

"For through him we both have access by one Spirit unto the Father. Now therefore ye are no more strangers and foreigners, but fellowcitizens with the saints, and of the household of God" (Eph. 2:18–19). Through the Lord Jesus Christ both Jew and Gentile have access to God the Father through the Holy Spirit, who dwells within us. How gracious of God to promise believers fellowship with Himself and with His saints. To think that we will have fellowship with the apostles and prophets and saints of old! How gracious God is to welcome us into His presence in loving fellowship with His people by the grace of the Lord Jesus Christ. Let us determine to walk in fellowship with Him here and now.

Golden thought: **We are fellow citizens with the saints in the household of God.**

"For by grace are ye saved through faith; and that not of yourselves: it is the gift of God" (Eph. 2:8).

April 10

"*But* unto every one of us is given grace according to the measure of the gift of Christ" (Eph. 4:7). The Lord Jesus Christ promises to every saint the gift of His grace. It is grace greater than our sin, grace that breaks the shackles of sin and sets us free to serve Christ as He desires. The Lord does not give grace in a miserly fashion; He pours it forth upon His people in bountiful supply. Everything He asks us to do in His Word He freely supplies the grace to accomplish. We need to consciously receive His grace and allow it to work in us mightily to produce obedience and fruit that will abound to the glory of God. By His grace we can accomplish all the will of God for our lives.

Golden thought: **To every one of us is given grace.**

"And be renewed in the spirit of your mind; and that ye put on the new man, which after God is created in righteousness and true holiness" (Eph. 4:23–24).

April 11

"*B*eing confident of this very thing, that he which hath begun a good work in you will perform it until the day of Jesus Christ" (Phil. 1:6). If you are a born again believer in Christ, you may be confident that the Lord Jesus Christ will complete what He has started in your life. In the consummation to come you will be shining with glory in His presence by His grace. Now we need to submit to His grace and allow Him to accomplish through us all that He wills. The apostle Paul constantly prayed for his converts. We need to be praying for one another that God may continue working in our lives that grace to live for Him. We need to allow Him to keep on molding us into His image to the glory of His Father.

_____

Golden thought: **He who began a good work in you will perform it.**

"Grace be unto you, and peace, from God the Father, and from the Lord Jesus Christ" (Phil. 1:2).

April 12

"*B*ehold, God is my salvation; I will trust, and not be afraid: for the Lord JEHOVAH is my strength and my song; he also is become my salvation" (Isa. 12:2). The believer should praise God for the greatness of His salvation. We must not be afraid of life or circumstances. God is all the strength we need. We ought to be continually singing His praises for the greatness of His love. We need to trust Him to guide us through our pathway safely to the home He is preparing for His saints. God has promised His people salvation in His presence; we should have serene trust in His ability to fulfill all that He has promised. We serve a great God. The day will come when we will be able to praise Him face to face.

_____

Golden thought: **I will trust and not be afraid, for the Lord is my strength.**

"Sing unto the Lord; for he hath done excellent things" (Isa. 12:5).

April 13

"*B*lessed be the Lord my strength . . . yea, happy is that people, whose God is the Lord" (Ps. 144:1, 15). The psalm begins and ends with a thought on the nature of God. It is the nature of God to be the strength of His people. When David was in trouble, he counted God as "my fortress; my high tower, and my deliverer" (v. 2). It is not the nature of God to stand by and watch His people being harmed without stretching forth His hand to protect and deliver them. The people who have such a God should indeed be happy and blessed. We should respond as David did to the promise of the nature of God: "I will sing a new song unto thee, O God" (v. 9). We too should be singing praise to the promise-keeping God.

Golden thought: **Happy is the people whose God is the Lord.**

"The Lord is good to all: and his tender mercies are over all his works" (Ps. 145:9).

April 14

"My grace is sufficient for thee: for my strength is made perfect in weakness" (II Cor. 12:9). The promise of the grace of God is all-sufficient for the believer. God's strength matches our weakness perfectly. We cannot serve God as we ought, but His grace enables us to stand on His promise and serve in His strength. The apostle Paul gloried in his infirmities because he knew that the power of Christ rested upon him to accomplish his ministry. We, too, must trust in the promise of the grace of God. If we need help in serving Christ, let us ask Him for it. If we are weak in our own strength, let us ask for His strength to accomplish the service He calls us to.

Golden thought: **Christ says, "My grace is sufficient for thee."**
"Most gladly therefore will I rather glory in my infirmities, that the power of Christ may rest upon me" (II Cor. 12:9).

April 15

"*M*any are the afflictions of the righteous: but the Lord delivereth him out of them all" (Ps. 34:19). God does not promise His people an easy path; He does promise them help at every step along the way. If we had no trouble, we would go through life with no thought of God at all. But we have many troubles and trials to endure. Thus, we have numerous opportunities to ask God for help and grace along the way. He is always listening and always ready to impart just the strength we need. Let us seek Him early; let us not wait until we are sinking to call upon Him for the help we need. He always delivers those who trust in Him, and one day He will deliver His people perfectly and permanently from all their trials to bring them to Himself.

Golden thought: **The Lord delivers His people from all trials.**

"This poor man cried, and the Lord heard him, and saved him out of all his troubles" (Ps. 34:6).

April 16

"For the hope which is laid up for you in heaven, whereof ye heard before in the word of the truth of the gospel" (Col. 1:5). The believer has a secure hope in the promise of heaven. This world is not the be all and end all of our lives. We trust in God's promise of eternal life in heaven, the place He is preparing for His people (John 14:3). The book of Revelation describes heaven as a place of ineffable beauty and loving fellowship between God and His people (Rev. 21:1–7). Our hearts must not be satisfied with this world; we must have our hearts set upon the promise of God of heaven in the world to come. The gospel does not merely save our souls here; it saves us for endless ages to come.

Golden thought: **Our hope is laid up for us in heaven.**

"If we hope for that we see not, then do we with patience wait for it" (Rom. 8:25).

April 17

"For we know that if our earthly house of this tabernacle were dissolved, we have a building of God, an house not made with hands, eternal in the heavens" (II Cor. 5:1). Our earthly tent house is plainly the physical body we now have. No one lives in a tent forever. If they should die, God assures His people that they have a heavenly house, the resurrection body, which is eternal and indestructible. The resurrection body of the Lord Jesus Christ is the example of what awaits the believer in the world to come. The resurrection body will be a perfect instrument with which to serve God for endless ages. It will never grow tired and will never wear out. The saints in glory will never be "slowed down" by the weakness of the flesh.

Golden thought: **We have a house not made with hands, eternal in the heavens.**

"Therefore, my beloved brethren, be ye stedfast, unmoveable, always abounding in the work of the Lord" (I Cor. 15:58).

April 18

"*T*he Lord knoweth how to deliver the godly out of temptations, and to reserve the unjust unto the day of judgment to be punished" (II Pet. 2:9). The Lord keeps all His promises. He will one day deliver all His redeemed people from the presence of sin and Satan and give them the joyous opportunity of fellowshiping together in His presence (Rev. 22:3–4). He will also summon the wicked to the bar of judgment and cast them out of His presence forever (Rev. 20:11–15). He will give to each one the precise recompense that the individual should have. Those who wish to be free from sin and forever in love with God will be satisfied perfectly. Those who choose sin ahead of God will be stuck with it forever.

Golden thought: **The Lord knows how to deliver the godly out of temptation.**

"And lead us not into temptation, but deliver us from evil" (Matt. 6:13).

April 19

"*For* I will give you a mouth and wisdom, which all your adversaries shall not be able to gainsay or resist" (Luke 21:15). In times of persecution believers do not have to write a speech to have a good testimony before their persecutors. Christ will impart the grace to stand to testify for Him to every faithful believer. The truth alone is a convicting testimony. Hard-hearted persecutors are often converted by such a simple and faithful testimony. Saul was convicted by Stephen's faithful testimony and ultimately converted and called to be an apostle (Acts 7:57–8:1). The Philippian jailor was convicted by the testimonies of Paul and Silas and was later converted (Acts 16:25–34).

Golden thought: **"I will give you a mouth and wisdom."**
"For from you sounded out the word of the Lord" (I Thess. 1:8).

April 20

"When wisdom entereth into thine heart, and knowledge is pleasant unto thy soul; discretion shall preserve thee, understanding shall keep thee" (Prov. 2:10–11). To have God's wisdom is a source of prudence and protection for every believer. No one wants to blunder into foolish or dangerous situations, but it is easy to do so if you rely on your own shrewdness. The wisdom of God's Word is an excellent protection. We all need to hide the Word in our hearts that we may find it there in times of trial. The psalmist could say, "I have more understanding than all my teachers: for thy testimonies are my meditation" (Ps. 119:99). We need to meditate on the wisdom and knowledge of the Word.

Golden thought: **When wisdom enters your heart, understanding guards you.**

"O how love I thy law! it is my meditation all the day" (Ps. 119:97).

April 21

"The grass withereth, the flower fadeth: but the word of our God shall stand for ever" (Isa. 40:8). The beauties of earth shall pass away, but the revelation of God in the Bible shall never pass away. God's people hide His Word in their hearts, and they shall have it there for all eternity. In the life to come the veil will be lifted, and they will remember all the precious promises of God and will realize that He has kept every one of them. Now it is our privilege to think of them and meditate on how much He has promised to His people. The day will come in which we will see the fulfillment for every one of them. How great is the love of God for His people!

Golden thought: **The word of our God shall stand forever.**

"Thy word have I hid in mine heart, that I might not sin against thee" (Ps. 119:11).

April 22

"He shall feed his flock like a shepherd: he shall gather the lambs with his arm, and carry them in his bosom, and shall gently lead those that are with young" (Isa. 40:11). The great Messiah, the Lord Jesus Christ, is often portrayed in Scripture as a shepherd who manifests loving care for his flock. He is especially gentle with children and others who need special care, such as expectant mothers. For all eternity He will be the Good Shepherd who cares for His flock. We may trust in His keeping power, for He will never abandon His people. He is leading us homeward to that place He is preparing for us. Let us walk the pathway with serene confidence in His care.

Golden thought: **"He shall feed his flock like a shepherd."**
"Surely goodness and mercy shall follow me all the days of my life: and I will dwell in the house of the Lord for ever" (Ps. 23:6).

April 23

"*B*ut they that wait upon the Lord shall renew their strength; they shall mount up with wings as eagles; they shall run, and not be weary; and they shall walk, and not faint" (Isa. 40:31). To wait on the Lord is to live a life of humble submission to the will of God, obeying His Word. They will discover that God continually strengthens them and upholds them. By His grace they will soar over what looked like insurmountable obstacles. They will run in obedience to His will and will not be exhausted. They will continually walk His pathway and will find that He sustains them every step of the way. They will not faint because the Good Shepherd constantly cares for them.

Golden thought: **They that wait on the Lord shall renew their strength.**

"For the Lord is a God of judgment: blessed are all they that wait for him" (Isa. 30:18).

April 24

"*I* am the good shepherd: the good shepherd giveth his life for the sheep" (John 10:11). The Lord Jesus Christ sacrificed Himself on the cross in order that He might save all who will believe in Him. Shepherds who care for their flock will risk their lives for the sheep, even as David faced the lion and the bear for his sheep (I Sam. 17:34–35). But the Lord Jesus died in order to save His people from their sins. No mere human being could do that. He was the divine Son of God, mighty to save. He laid down His life for the sheep and took it again in resurrection power (John 10:17–18). We should walk in serene confidence in the keeping power of our great Shepherd.

Golden thought: **Jesus said, "I am the good shepherd."**
"My sheep hear my voice, and I know them, and they follow me" (John 10:27).

April 25

"*B*ut ye shall receive power, after that the Holy Ghost is come upon you: and ye shall be witnesses unto me both in Jerusalem, and in all Judaea, and in Samaria, and unto the uttermost part of the earth" (Acts 1:8). The Lord Jesus left this promise with His people before He ascended back to His Father. It remains the marching orders of His church and a most precious promise of empowerment in proclaiming the gospel message. The Lord Jesus is the Savior of the world and we are called upon to make Him known to all who will listen. We never stand alone. His Holy Spirit enables us to testify for Him that others may learn of His saving grace. Tell them that Jesus saves!

Golden thought: **You shall be witnesses unto Me.**

"And daily in the temple, and in every house, they ceased not to teach and preach Jesus Christ" (Acts 5:42).

April 26

"And when the chief Shepherd shall appear, ye shall receive a crown of glory that fadeth not away" (I Pet. 5:4). Peter is addressing the elders of the flock, but there can be no doubt that God will reward the faithful service of every believer as well. The elders must feed the flock of God with the wholesome food of the Word. But all the saints can share their knowledge of the Word with their friends and neighbors. The Lord will not overlook a single thing that is done for Him. We must all be zealous in living for that heavenly realm rather than the tawdry baubles of the present world. We must keep the upward look, living for Jesus in this present world, that He might be pleased with our service.

Golden thought: **You shall receive a crown of glory.**
"But the end of all things is at hand: be ye therefore sober, and watch unto prayer" (I Pet. 4:7).

April 27

"Casting all your care upon him; for he careth for you" (I Pet. 5:7). The thought refers back to the command in v. 6, "Humble yourselves therefore under the mighty hand of God." If we put ourselves in humble submission to God, we may have supreme confidence in His keeping power. Any trials or worries that arise in the path of doing God's will may be cast upon Him. He will see to it that His will is done and His faithful servant is sustained and blessed. The believer should never worry over circumstances when he is obedient to God's revealed will in Scripture. We should not overlook the word *all*. God will take care of the little annoyances as well as the great problems that His servants may face.

Golden thought: **He cares for you.**

"Be careful for nothing; but in every thing by prayer and supplication with thanksgiving let your requests be made known unto God" (Phil. 4:6).

April 28

"And many of them that sleep in the dust of the earth shall awake, some to everlasting life, and some to shame and everlasting contempt. And they that be wise shall shine as the brightness of the firmament; and they that turn many to righteousness as the stars for ever and ever" (Dan. 12:2–3). Daniel prophesies a coming resurrection of both the righteous and the wicked. He promises shame and eternal contempt for the wicked, for they have spurned God's promises. But for the righteous He promises glory, for they have received God's promises and will shine like the stars forever and ever. All men should choose God's promises and stake everything upon them.

Golden thought: **"They that be wise shall shine as the brightness of the firmament."**

"There is one glory of the sun, and another glory of the moon, and another glory of the stars. . . . So also is the resurrection of the dead" (I Cor. 15:41–42).

April 29

"And I will pour upon the house of David, and upon the inhabitants of Jerusalem, the spirit of grace and of supplications: and they shall look upon me whom they have pierced, and they shall mourn for him, as one mourneth for his only son, and shall be in bitterness for him, as one that is in bitterness for his firstborn" (Zech. 12:10). During the Tribulation period the Lord will pour out His grace upon His earthly people, the Jews. There will be a national conversion as Zechariah describes. They will be powerful witnesses for the Lord Jesus (Rev. 7:4–17). The converted and restored nation will lead the millennial nations in the true worship of Jehovah God (Zech. 14:16).

Golden thought: **"They shall look upon me whom they have pierced."**

"And so all Israel shall be saved: as it is written, There shall come out of Sion the Deliverer, and shall turn away ungodliness from Jacob" (Rom. 11:26).

April 30

"*B*ut unto you that fear my name shall the Sun of righteousness arise with healing in his wings" (Mal. 4:2). The word *fear* denotes the proper reverence that puts the Lord first in the life. This is a glorious messianic promise of the Lord Jesus Christ, whose miracles of healing were outstanding in the public ministry of His first advent (Matt. 9:35). But the apostle John saw the Lord Jesus in glory "and his countenance was as the sun shineth in his strength" (Rev. 1:16). Malachi foresaw the great kingdom reign when the Lord would remove the wicked from His kingdom (Mal. 4:3). The Lord Jesus taught the same thing in His Olivet Discourse (Matt. 25:31–46). "Even so, come, Lord Jesus" (Rev. 22:20).

Golden thought: **"The Sun of righteousness shall arise with healing in his wings."**

"Rejoice greatly, O daughter of Zion; shout, O daughter of Jerusalem: behold thy King cometh unto thee: he is just, and having salvation" (Zech. 9:9).

May 1

"*C*onsider the lilies of the field, how they grow; they toil not, neither do they spin: and yet I say unto you, that even Solomon in all his glory was not arrayed like one of these. Wherefore, if God so clothe the grass of the field, which to day is, and to morrow is cast into the oven, shall he not much more clothe you, O ye of little faith?" (Matt. 6:28–30). The splendor of the spring flowers is a beautiful reminder of the providential care of God for His people. "Therefore take no thought, saying, What shall we eat? or, What shall we drink? or Wherewithal shall we be clothed? . . . for your heavenly Father knoweth that ye have need of all these things" (Matt. 6:31–32). A loving God will provide for all our needs.

———————————

Golden thought: **Shall not God much more clothe you?**

"But seek ye first the kingdom of God, and his righteousness" (Matt. 6:33).

May 2

"*B*ehold the fowls of the air: for they sow not, neither do they reap, nor gather into barns; yet your heavenly Father feedeth them. Are ye not much better than they?" (Matt. 6:26). The birds and other wildlife are an excellent example of God's provision for His creation. God cares for all His creatures. Surely He will care for His people as well. "Therefore I say unto you, Take no [anxious] thought for your life, what ye shall eat, or what ye shall drink; nor yet for your body, what ye shall put on. Is not the life more than meat, and the body than raiment?" (Matt. 6:25). God will provide for His people's needs. We need to walk by faith and trust Him for all our needs.

Golden thought: **Are you not much better than the birds?**
"I can do all things through Christ which strengtheneth me" (Phil. 4:13).

May 3

"For God so loved the world, that he gave his only begotten Son, that whosoever believeth in him should not perish, but have everlasting life" (John 3:16). God the Father gave His dear Son, the Lord Jesus Christ, that this sinful world might be saved by trusting in His death for sin upon the cross. It was infinite love that gave such a gift. Without Christ's sacrifice, the whole world would perish in their sins. But His death upon the cross atoned for the sins of the whole world. Now, whoever receives Christ as Savior has everlasting life with Him. If you, the reader, have not received Him as your Savior, now is the right time to do so. He alone can blot out all your sins. Pray and ask Him!

Golden thought: **God so loved that He gave His Son.**
"He that believeth on him is not condemned" (John 3:18).

May 4

"He that believeth on the Son hath everlasting life: and he that believeth not the Son shall not see life; but the wrath of God abideth on him" (John 3:36). The person who believes on the Lord Jesus Christ for salvation *has*, not *will have*, eternal life. God imparts His life to the believer. The absence of life is not extinction but the wrath of God. Man is a living soul and must live somewhere forever. The love of God the Father rests on His dear Son, the Lord Jesus Christ, and upon all those who trust in Him for their eternal salvation. Eternal life is not mere existence but loving fellowship with the Father and with His Son our Savior, Jesus Christ.

Golden thought: **He who believes on the Son has eternal life.**

"The Father judgeth no man, but hath committed all judgment unto the Son" (John 5:22).

May 5

"*I*f my people, which are called by my name, shall humble themselves, and pray, and seek my face, and turn from their wicked ways; then will I hear from heaven, and will forgive their sin, and will heal their land" (II Chron. 7:14). Not only lost sinners but sometimes God's people also get out of fellowship with Him and need to get right. If they will humble themselves and ask His forgiveness, God is quick to forgive and restore them. God is always aware of the prayers of His people (v. 15). There are times when we need to rededicate ourselves to His will and His service. All who seek His face will find Him and will discover how gracious and loving He is.

Golden thought: **If My people will seek My face, I will hear and forgive.**

"Truly our fellowship is with the Father, and with His Son Jesus Christ" (I John 1:3).

May 6

"*B*ut whosoever drinketh of the water that I shall give him shall never thirst; but the water that I shall give him shall be in him a well of water springing up into everlasting life" (John 4:14). The Lord Jesus told the Samaritan woman that He was the water of life and the Jewish Messiah (v. 26). She believed His word and found out that it was true. She was quick to tell others about the great salvation that she had found in Him (v. 39). The result was that many of the Samaritans believed in Him as the Savior of the world (vv. 40–42). Every believer needs to drink deeply of the water of life that flows from the grace of the Lord Jesus Christ. He is an artesian well of living water.

Golden thought: **Whoever drinks of the water that Jesus gives shall never thirst.**

"And whosoever will, let him take the water of life freely" (Rev. 22:17).

May 7

"*I* am the living bread which came down from heaven: if any man eat of this bread, he shall live for ever: and the bread that I will give is my flesh, which I will give for the life of the world" (John 6:51). The Lord Jesus explained that He was about to die for the sins of the world. His death would mean life for all those who receive Him as their personal Savior. He did not die as a martyr but as the divine Son of God, atoning for the sins of the world. The idea of *eating* Him refers to receiving Him as the only Savior of the world. Salvation in Christ means eternal life by His grace. In the ancient world bread was regarded as the staff of life. It was the staple diet for every meal.

Golden thought: **Jesus said, "I am the living bread."**
"As the living Father hath sent me, and I live by the Father: so he that eateth me, even he shall live by me" (John 6:57).

May 8

"*H*e that believeth on me, as the scripture hath said, out of his belly shall flow rivers of living water" (John 7:38). Believing in Christ makes the believer a source of refreshment for all others. Because he is saved by Christ, he can tell others how to be saved as well. His life can become a blessing to all those about him. The sustaining life that Christ pours into the believer can become a source of salvation and refreshment to others about him. Only eternity will reveal how many people the believer has influenced for Christ. We need to pray for others about us, that our testimony may be a real help to their eternal souls. Share the blessing.

Golden thought: **Out of the believer shall flow rivers of living water.**

Jesus said, "If any man thirst, let him come unto me, and drink" (John 7:37).

May 9

"Thy words were found, and I did eat them; and thy word was unto me the joy and rejoicing of mine heart: for I am called by thy name, O Lord God of hosts" (Jer. 15:16). The reading of and meditation on Scripture is like the eating and digestion of food. Scripture promises food for the soul to believers who will think about the precious truths in it. As Jeremiah meditated on God's Word, he found joy in the promises of the Almighty. Today also believers need to *chew* upon the promises of God's Word that the strength of God might fill their hearts to serve Him in this generation. Meditation on Scripture should not be a lost art in our generation. "How sweet are thy words unto my taste! yea, sweeter than honey to my mouth" (Ps. 119:103).

Golden thought: **Your Word was unto me the joy and rejoicing of my heart.**

"O how love I thy law! it is my meditation all the day" (Ps. 119:97).

May 10

"Then spake Jesus again unto them, saying, I am the light of the world: he that followeth me shall not walk in darkness, but shall have the light of life" (John 8:12). The Lord Jesus shines with great splendor in the hearts of His people, but He is also the light of the whole world. Whoever will look to Him will find the light of salvation shining in his heart. Those who receive Him as their Savior will find the light of His presence illuminating their pathway. Lost people walk in darkness and can see no way out, but those who come to Jesus and receive Him as Savior have the light of God shining in their hearts. We must continue walking in the light of His presence every day.

Golden thought: **Jesus said, "I am the light of the world."**
"The darkness is past, and the true light now shineth" (I John 2:8).

May 11

"Then said Jesus to those Jews which believed on him, If ye continue in my word, then are ye my disciples indeed; and ye shall know the truth, and the truth shall make you free" (John 8:31–32). Some people read a little bit about Jesus and then fly away to other ideas. But those who believe in His Word and continue learning more will come to a clear knowledge of the truth of God. The Lord Jesus manifested the truth of God in His life and teaching. Those who are committed to Him find that His truth breaks the shackles of error and darkness. Instead of slaving for sin, the believer is free to serve God as he desires from the heart. We must continue searching the Scriptures.

Golden thought: **"The truth shall make you free."**
Jesus said, "I am the way, the truth, and the life" (John 14:6).

May 12

"*I* am the door: by me if any man enter in, he shall be saved, and shall go in and out, and find pasture" (John 10:9). The Lord Jesus Christ is the only door to eternal salvation. To enter into the Father's presence, the believer must go through the Lord Jesus as his door, his access to God the Father. The Lord's promise is clear: He shall be saved. But heaven is not a trap: there is freedom in salvation; he shall go in and out. There is also sustenance in the presence of God: he shall find pasture. All the needs of the faithful sheep will be met by the loving Shepherd. If He gave His life for the sheep, He will not withhold any other good thing. Have you entered by the Door?

Golden thought: **Jesus said, "I am the door."**
"Having therefore, brethren, boldness to enter into the holiest by the blood of Jesus" (Heb. 10:19).

May 13

"*J*esus said unto her, I am the resurrection and the life: he that believeth in me, though he were dead, yet shall he live" (John 11:25). The words of the Lord Jesus to Martha have profound comfort to all believers as well. The Lord Jesus not only would raise up Lazarus for Martha but He also will raise up all the dead who die in the Lord. But at the resurrection He will not merely restore the dead to physical life but will give them resurrection bodies that are incorruptible (I Cor. 15:42). The key is faith in the Lord Jesus Christ. Martha had to trust in His word, and every believer must trust in the Lord for his own salvation and glorification. The Lord Jesus is everything to His trusting saints.

Golden thought: **Jesus said, "I am the resurrection and the life."**
"That I may know him, and the power of his resurrection, and the fellowship of his sufferings" (Phil. 3:10).

May 14

"*F*or I know that my redeemer liveth, and that he shall stand at the latter day upon the earth: and though after my skin worms destroy this body, yet in my flesh shall I see God" (Job 19:25–26). Job speaks as a trusting believer in the resurrection power of his Savior and Redeemer. Although he suffered in this life, he was sure that the Lord would raise him up at the day of resurrection. But we also know that the Lord delivered him from his afflictions and restored his goods and herds. The Lord also gave him more children as an added blessing. None of us should be discouraged by sad circumstances. The Lord is in control and will work out all things for the benefit of His people.

Golden thought: **I know that my Redeemer lives.**
"This Jesus hath God raised up, whereof we all are witnesses" (Acts 2:32).

May 15

"God shall judge the righteous and the wicked: for there is a time there for every purpose and for every work" (Eccles. 3:17). God has created every human being as a morally responsible person. Every person needs to recognize that there is a day of accountability coming. God shall judge every human being according to his works. God shall examine every purpose and every work. The righteous shall be rewarded, and the wicked shall be condemned. That is why the sacrifice of the Lord Jesus upon the cross is so important. "For when we were yet without strength, in due time Christ died for the ungodly" (Rom. 5:6). "But God commendeth his love toward us, in that, while we were yet sinners, Christ died for us" (Rom. 5:8).

Golden thought: **"God shall judge the righteous and the wicked."**
"Let not sin therefore reign in your mortal body, that ye should obey it in the lusts thereof" (Rom. 6:12).

May 16

"*For* he remembered his holy promise, and Abraham his servant" (Ps. 105:42). God's promise is a solemn and sacred thing. God always remembers His promises. He had promised to Abraham that He would lead His people out of Egypt into the Promised Land. He did so with mighty power in the plagues upon Egypt (Ps. 105:28–34). He brought water from the rock for them in the wilderness (Ps. 105:41). God brought forth His people with joy and gave them the lands of the heathen (Ps. 105:43–44). We should also remember His promises and claim them by the merits of Jesus Christ. We should be His servants that His promises might be fulfilled in us.

Golden thought: **God remembered His holy promise.**

"Seek the Lord, and his strength: seek his face evermore" (Ps. 105:4).

May 17

"*T*hat ye be not slothful, but followers of them who through faith and patience inherit the promises" (Heb. 6:12). Believers must put themselves in the place of obedient servants of God. We, too, must trust God as the saints of old did. We must patiently wait for the fulfillment of His Word as they did. God does not hurry in accomplishing His will, but He always keeps His promises. We must patiently trust Him to keep all His promises in due time. There is still much in God's Word that we have not absorbed. We need to continue searching the Scriptures that we might understand and obey them in a better way. Then we will see more of His promises fulfilled.

———————————————

Golden thought: **Be followers of them who through faith and patience inherit the promises.**

"Sanctify them through thy truth: thy word is truth" (John 17:17).

May 18

"*B*lessed be the Lord, that hath given rest unto his people Israel, according to all that he promised: there hath not failed one word of all his good promise, which he promised by the hand of Moses his servant" (I Kings 8:56). Solomon's word of blessing at the dedication of the temple praises God's faithfulness to His promises. We too need to pause to thank God for His faithfulness to His promises to us. We too have often stumbled in our obedience to His Word, but God always keeps His promises to us. We can echo Solomon's prayer, "The Lord our God be with us, as he was with our fathers: let him not leave us, nor forsake us: that he may incline our hearts unto him, to walk in all his ways" (I Kings 8:57–58).

Golden thought: **There has not failed one word of all God's good promise.**

"Let your heart therefore be perfect with the Lord our God, to walk in his statutes" (I Kings 8:61).

May 19

"*B*elieve on the Lord Jesus Christ, and thou shalt be saved, and thy house" (Acts 16:31). Paul and Silas gave the Word of the Lord to the Philippian jailor, and part of it was this great promise of salvation to all who will believe in Christ. The Lord Jesus paid our debt by His sufferings on the cross; there is nothing left for us to do but to receive Him as Savior and trust in His keeping power to bring us to His heavenly Father. Once we are saved, we can do things that please Him, as the Philippian jailor did (Acts 16:33–34). But it is the sacrifice of Christ alone that brings us salvation. We should trust in His Word alone to save us and bring us to God.

Golden thought: **Believe on the Lord Jesus Christ and you shall be saved.**

"The wages of sin is death; but the gift of God is eternal life through Jesus Christ our Lord" (Rom. 6:23).

May 20

"The Lord will give strength unto his people; the Lord will bless his people with peace" (Ps. 29:11). The Lord is all-powerful and delights in providing strength for His people. We must resist the temptation to accomplish things in our own strength and rather learn how to draw upon the strength of the Lord. He can impart to His people the sustaining grace that will enable them to serve Him well. Too often we get that harried and frazzled feeling of trying too hard to serve the Lord. We need to slow down to draw upon His strength and wisdom to serve Him well. There is great peace to those who serve in the strength of the Lord and let Him guide their steps.

Golden thought: **The Lord will give strength to His people.**
"For thou art the God of my strength" (Ps. 43:2).

May 21

"Whatsoever a man soweth, that shall he also reap. For he that soweth to his flesh shall of the flesh reap corruption; but he that soweth to the Spirit shall of the Spirit reap life everlasting" (Gal. 6:7–8). The person who continues sowing to his sinful nature will soon discover that he has a boa constrictor around him. On the other hand, a person who systematically sows to the spirit in Bible study and prayer will discover that the Spirit of God has broken the shackles of sin and set him free to serve God in a better and larger way. There is a spiritual harvest in the obedient believer's life that will be a blessing to him and to all who know him. And there is life everlasting that follows.

Golden thought: **He who sows to the Spirit shall of the Spirit reap life everlasting.**

"But the fruit of the Spirit is love, joy, peace, longsuffering, gentleness, goodness, faith, meekness, temperance" (Gal. 5:22–23).

May 22

"For this God is our God for ever and ever: he will be our guide even unto death" (Ps. 48:14). The psalmist claimed the God of the Bible as his God. Every believer should commit himself to God the same way. God will be our God forever. He never changes and will never fail us. He will be our guide through all of life. Every decision can be made on the basis of God's guidance in His Word. But God will not only guide us through this life, He will be our Guide forever and ever. For all eternity we will be following that same God who has provided loving care for us throughout this life. How great are His kindness and grace to His people! Let us follow His leading and guidance with zeal.

Golden thought: **God will be our Guide.**

"But ever follow that which is good, both among yourselves, and to all men" (I Thess. 5:15).

May 23

"God resisteth the proud, but giveth grace unto the humble" (James 4:6). Those who think that they are self-sufficient and need no help from God certainly will not receive any help from Him. God will stand in the way of the proud man to defeat his purpose. But God pours out grace upon those who seek His face and ask for help. Every believer needs to walk humbly with God, obeying biblical teaching and seeking to please God in all his ways. God delights in lifting up the humble and enlarging his service for the Almighty. All believers need God's help and should humbly ask Him for it. The Lord is prepared to give far more than we can ask.

_____

Golden thought: **God gives grace to the humble.**
"What doth the Lord require of thee, but to do justly, and to love mercy, and to walk humbly with thy God?" (Mic. 6:8).

May 24

"*F*or if ye live after the flesh, ye shall die: but if ye through the Spirit do mortify the deeds of the body, ye shall live" (Rom. 8:13). There is a life and death struggle going on for the life of every person. If the person surrenders to the lusts of the flesh, he is on a downward path that will lead to eternal death, not extinction but loss of spiritual life. But if the individual allows the Spirit of God to put to death the deeds of the body, that person will live forever in the presence of God. Self-sacrifice is a noble thing if it puts the Spirit of God on the throne of the life. That battle of putting the Spirit in control is worth fighting. The believer wins by surrendering to the Spirit of God.

Golden thought: **Through the Spirit you shall live.**

"For as many as are led by the Spirit of God, they are the sons of God" (Rom. 8:14).

May 25

"*B*ut other fell into good ground, and brought forth fruit, some an hundredfold, some sixtyfold, some thirtyfold" (Matt. 13:8). In the act of sowing seed there is a promise of a harvest. No farmer sows a seed in the hope of getting just one seed back. He hopes for an abundant harvest. So the soulwinner who sows the seed of the Word should expect an abundant harvest. It is not his great ability that is important. He hopes for the promise of the seed of the Word to bring forth fruit. God can bless His Word in the lives of those who hear so that it brings forth much fruit. It is a comfort to Christian workers to know the mysteries of the kingdom of heaven (Matt. 13:11).

Golden thought: **"Other fell into good ground, and brought forth fruit."**

"Being born again, not of corruptible seed, but of incorruptible, by the word of God, which liveth and abideth for ever" (I Pet. 1:23).

May 26

"For ever, O Lord, thy word is settled in heaven" (Ps. 119:89). The Word of God is imperishable. Wicked men have burned Bibles and persecuted God's believers, but none have been able to keep the Word of God from spreading abroad around the world. God has settled His Word in heaven and is using His servants to spread the message on earth. The Word of God is a divinely inspired message of salvation to all who will believe. God promises that He will not allow His Word to perish from the earth. Every time we share the Word with others we are sharing in God's promise of the eternal testimony of His holy Word. Sow the seed of the Word boldly!

Golden thought: **The word of our God is settled forever.**

"Ye shall be witnesses unto me" (Acts 1:8).

May 27

"And it shall come to pass, that whosoever shall call upon the name of the Lord shall be delivered: for in mount Zion and in Jerusalem shall be deliverance, as the Lord hath said, and in the remnant whom the Lord shall call" (Joel 2:32). Joel prophesies the coming persecution of the Jewish remnant in the day of the Lord, the Tribulation period. When they call upon the Lord for help, the Lord will deliver them. This is a timeless promise that is based on the unchangeable nature of God. He always helps those who call upon Him in sincerity. We should call upon God for help in time of need. He is listening.

Golden thought: **"Whosoever shall call upon the name of the Lord shall be delivered."**

"The Lord will hear when I call unto him" (Ps. 4:3).

May 28

"And it shall come to pass, that whosoever shall call upon the name of the Lord shall be saved" (Acts 2:21). On the day of Pentecost the apostle Peter quoted Joel 2:32 and applied it universally to those who should believe and be saved. Anyone who hears the promises of God's Word and calls upon the Lord Jesus for salvation will be heard. God is prepared to save all who trust in the Lord Jesus for their salvation. If you, the reader, have never done this, you ought to bow your head right now to ask God to forgive you your sins and save you for Jesus' sake. Works cannot save you. Only Jesus can save. But now you need to live a life of obedience to Him and His Word to show that you are saved.

Golden thought: **Whoever calls upon the name of the Lord shall be saved.**

"I will call upon the Lord, who is worthy to be praised" (Ps. 18:3).

May 29

"And he shall be like a tree planted by the rivers of water, that bringeth forth his fruit in his season; his leaf also shall not wither; and whatsoever he doeth shall prosper" (Ps. 1:3). The man who delights in his law of the Lord and meditates in God's Word daily shall prosper in his spiritual life. His relationship to the Lord will deepen and strengthen as he walks according to God's Word. The fruit of godly living will become manifest to others. In the Middle East water is scarce; people come to admire trees that grow near streams of water. In the same way, people will notice those who live by God's Word and manifest submission to the will of God. People can recognize spiritual prosperity.

Golden thought: **"Whatsoever he doeth shall prosper."**
"For the Lord knoweth the way of the righteous: but the way of the ungodly shall perish" (Ps. 1:6).

May 30

"According as his divine power hath given unto us all things that pertain unto life and godliness . . . whereby are given unto us exceeding great and precious promises: that by these ye might be partakers of the divine nature, having escaped the corruption that is in the world through lust" (II Pet. 1:3–4). God has graciously supplied our needs through His Word. His promises move us toward His love, sustaining grace, and spiritual power. Through His promises we can escape the corruption that is defiling the world. Worldly people destroy one another through their greed and lust for things. God promises all we need for our journey through this world. His grace is sufficient for us.

Golden thought: **His divine power has given us all things that pertain to life.**

"And besides this, giving all diligence, add to your faith virtue" (II Pet. 1:5).

May 31

"Then they that feared the Lord spake often one to another: and the Lord hearkened. . . . And they shall be mine, saith the Lord of hosts, in that day when I make up my jewels; and I will spare them, as a man spareth his own son that serveth him" (Mal. 3:16–17). The Lord is listening when His saints try to strengthen and encourage one another by His Word. He claims them as His jewels, which He will display one day in that glorious realm He is preparing for His people. He takes special care of them, for He intends to cherish them forever. We should take pains to help the brethren because they are very important people to the Lord.

———————————

Golden thought: **God says, "They shall be mine . . . when I make up my jewels."**

"The fear of the Lord is the beginning of wisdom" (Ps. 111:10).

June 1

"The Lord hath been mindful of us: he will bless us . . . He will bless them that fear the Lord, both small and great" (Ps. 115:12–13). The Lord does manifest tender care for His people. His blessing rests upon all His people, whoever they are. We should think of the Lord's blessing and ask for it upon all our service for Him. No one can reverence God from his heart without the Lord noticing it. God's blessing rests upon the lay people who serve by their witnessing, praying, and giving. His blessing rests upon the pastors and evangelists as they preach and teach the Word. God is pleased to bless the people who reverence His name in all their activities. Let us be zealous to reverence God above all.

Golden thought: **He will bless them that fear the Lord.**
"Ye that fear the Lord, trust in the Lord: he is their help and their shield" (Ps. 115:11).

June 2

"As ye are partakers of the sufferings, so shall ye be also of the consolation" (II Cor. 1:7). The apostle Paul had to suffer much, but he also had great consolation. Anytime we as believers are called upon to suffer, we must remember that there is great consolation as well. The Corinthians had to suffer, but they had the joy of seeing the gospel triumph throughout the province of Asia. God always sees to it that there is consolation for His people. We may be called to suffer many things, but God is always with His people and upholds them through all their trials. His presence is the greatest consolation that we can have, and it is one that will never be withdrawn.

Golden thought: **As we have sufferings, so we have consolation from God.**

"Thy rod and thy staff they comfort me" (Ps. 23:4).

June 3

"*F*or all the promises of God in him are yea, and in him Amen, unto the glory of God by us" (II Cor. 1:20). The fulfillment of God's promises is sure. He has given His Word and He shall do it. In the Lord Jesus Christ all the promises of God find their fulfillment. Christ honors His Father by fulfilling His promises. The apostle Paul, and all other faithful Christian workers, are simply being obedient to God's promises in proclaiming His Word to the nations. Hearing the Word gives men the opportunity to believe the promises and to seek God's fulfillment in His Word. Their fulfillment one by one gives glory to God through the Lord Jesus Christ.

Golden thought: **All the promises of God in Christ are yea and amen.**

"And the Lord gave Solomon wisdom, as he promised him" (I Kings 5:12).

June 4

"For when we were yet without strength, in due time Christ died for the ungodly" (Rom. 5:6). Perhaps someone might die for a good person (Rom. 5:7), but Christ died for us when we were reprobates. There is the promise of salvation for the wicked. No man can deserve it; it is a gracious gift of God. "But God commendeth his love toward us, in that, while we were yet sinners, Christ died for us" (Rom. 5:8). It is our place to receive that free gift and respond with thankful obedience to the loving promises of God. We can never repay that gift, but we can certainly worship Him and seek to serve Him in obedience to His holy Word. His grace will sustain us.

Golden thought: **Christ died for the ungodly.**

"Let not sin therefore reign in your mortal body, that ye should obey it in the lusts thereof" (Rom. 6:12).

June 5

"*B*ut if the wicked will turn from all his sins that he hath committed, and keep all my statutes, and do that which is lawful and right, he shall surely live, he shall not die" (Ezek. 18:21). Getting right with God requires a conversion: a turning from what is evil to what is right, God Himself. A person must submit to the Spirit of God's making a change in his heart and life. He needs to fill his mind with the Word of God that it may provide direction to his steps. He needs to seek out God's people and identify himself with a Bible-believing church. By the grace of God he needs to become a different person. God must become supreme in his life. God's Word must become the most important thing he possesses.

Golden thought: **"If the wicked will turn, . . . he shall surely live."**
"Thou hast turned for me my mourning into dancing: thou hast put off my sackcloth, and girded me with gladness" (Ps. 30:11).

June 6

"*T*he law of the Lord is perfect, converting the soul: the testimony of the Lord is sure, making wise the simple" (Ps. 19:7). The teaching of Scripture is powerful enough to change the soul of the person reading it. It can turn thoughts of wickedness into thoughts of God. It can change a simple-minded person into one filled with the wisdom of God. It can change the direction of a person's life from hell to heaven. But there must be a heart submission to what Scripture teaches. The reader needs to recognize the Bible, not as just another book but as God's divine revelation to mankind, a book of transforming power. We need to search the Scriptures for His truth.

Golden thought: **"The law of the Lord is perfect, converting the soul."**

"Let the words of my mouth, and the meditation of my heart, be acceptable in thy sight, O Lord, my strength, and my redeemer" (Ps. 19:14).

June 7

"*T*rust in the Lord with all thine heart; and lean not unto thine own understanding. In all thy ways acknowledge him, and he shall direct thy paths" (Prov. 3:5–6). The believer needs to forsake confidence in his own plans and become open to the leading of God in Scripture. If we trust in God and look to Him for guidance, He will give us the guidance we need in His Word. His instruction, His warnings, His revelation in Scripture provide the very guidance that we need day by day. We need to trust the Lord and His Word and look to the Scriptures for daily guidance on our pathway. His pathway always leads home.

Golden thought: **"Trust in the Lord with all thine heart . . . and He shall direct thy paths."**

"Come ye, and let us walk in the light of the Lord" (Isa. 2:5).

June 8

"*K*eep sound wisdom and discretion . . . then shalt thou walk in thy way safely, and thy foot shall not stumble" (Prov. 3:21, 23). Obedience to God's Word and submission to His wisdom are the proper pathway for every believer. When we walk in His pathway, we do not stumble. It is when we go our own willful direction that we find the stumbling stones and pitfalls. Our crafty plans are often ruined, but His pathway is perfect. There are no shortcuts to walking God's pathway. Searching the Scriptures and then faithfully walking that pathway are always the right way for the believer. God's blessing and God's presence attend the faithful walk of the believer.

Golden thought: **"Thy foot shall not stumble."**
"When thou goest, thy steps shall not be straitened; and when thou runnest, thou shalt not stumble" (Prov. 4:12).

June 9

"When thou liest down, thou shalt not be afraid: yea, thou shalt lie down, and thy sleep shall be sweet" (Prov. 3:24). Walking in God's pathway, according to His will, imparts a sense of peace and tranquility to the life that nothing else can bring. When you come to the end of the day, you can lie down and rest in serene peace, regardless of the tumult of the day that you had to walk through. God has been with you all the day, and His presence shall guard you at night as well. No man-made bomb shelter can impart the sense of peace and safety such as the presence of God can provide for the believer. Meditation upon Him brings peace and restful sleep.

Golden thought: **When you lie down, your sleep shall be sweet.**
"Return unto thy rest, O my soul; for the Lord hath dealt bountifully with thee" (Ps. 116:7).

June 10

"*B*ut the Lord is faithful, who shall stablish you, and keep you from evil" (II Thess. 3:3). The believer can always rest in the unchangeableness of God's faithfulness. He will establish the believer by His Word and will protect the believer from all evil. The believer should fill his heart and memory with the Scriptures so that God can bring them to his memory and guide him by their counsel. His grace can guard the believer from harm along dangerous pathways. The presence of the Lord is always the greatest protection the believer can have. We need to walk obediently and trustfully with God along our pathway. He can bring us safely home.

Golden thought: **"The Lord is faithful."**

"The grace of our Lord Jesus Christ be with you all. Amen."
(II Thess. 3:18).

June 11

"Whosoever transgresseth, and abideth not in the doctrine of Christ, hath not God. He that abideth in the doctrine of Christ, he hath both the Father and the Son" (II John 9). A person who denies the deity of Christ denies the biblical doctrine of the triune God. The believer who worships Christ as the divine Son of God has both Christ and the Father. The Father is so pleased that believers honor and worship His Son that He abides in the heart of the believer as well. You cannot dishonor the Father by honoring His dear Son. We may enter into loving fellowship with God through our Savior, the Lord Jesus Christ. Through Christ we may praise and worship each of the three Persons of the one true God.

———————————

Golden thought: **He that abides in the doctrine of Christ has fellowship with the Father.**

Jesus said, "I am the way, the truth, and the life: no man cometh unto the Father, but by me" (John 14:6).

June 12

"For God giveth to a man that is good in his sight wisdom, and knowledge, and joy: but to the sinner he giveth travail" (Eccles. 2:26). God loves to impart good gifts to His children. Through His Word, the Bible, he imparts wisdom and knowledge to those who search the Scriptures. But along with spiritual wisdom, He imparts the joy of His fellowship as well. There is nothing sweeter than the joy of feasting on the precious truths of His Word and having the knowledge of His good pleasure resting upon us. We can commune with the Author of the Book and rejoice in the truths that we see in His holy Word. But to the sinner there is nothing but trouble, for he spurns God's holy Word.

Golden thought: **God gives to His children wisdom, knowledge, and joy.**

"Wise men lay up knowledge: but the mouth of the foolish is near destruction" (Prov. 10:14).

June 13

"The Lord is nigh unto them that are of a broken heart; and saveth such as be of a contrite spirit" (Ps. 34:18). There are times when the believer feels that he has failed the Lord. That is not the time to hide from the Lord but to come and beg forgiveness. The Lord is ready to receive those who are brokenhearted over their sin and failure. He saves those who are contrite and seek His forgiveness through the Lord Jesus Christ. "Wherefore he is able also to save them to the uttermost that come unto God by him, seeing he ever liveth to make intercession for them" (Heb. 7:25). Through the intercession of the Lord Jesus, we have boldness to come before God to ask for forgiveness and cleansing.

Golden thought: **The Lord saves those who are contrite.**

"The Lord redeemeth the soul of his servants: and none of them that trust in him shall be desolate" (Ps. 34:22).

June 14

"*F*or if we believe that Jesus died and rose again, even so them also which sleep in Jesus will God bring with him" (I Thess. 4:14). The believer should look forward to the blessed hope of the second coming of the Lord Jesus Christ for His saints. It is just as sure as the death and resurrection of the Lord Jesus. We do not look forward to death, even though that is a possibility. We look forward to seeing the Lord Himself. When He comes for His saints, He will bring with Him those who have died in the past who are His redeemed people. There will be a glorious reunion in loving fellowship and worship of the Lord. How wonderful it will be to have fellowship with "the spirits of just men made perfect" (Heb. 12:23).

Golden thought: **Those who sleep in Jesus will God bring with Him.**

"Wherefore comfort one another with these words" (I Thess. 4:18).

June 15

"For none of us liveth to himself, and no man dieth to himself. For whether we live, we live unto the Lord; and whether we die, we die unto the Lord: whether we live therefore, or die, we are the Lord's" (Rom. 14:7–8). The believer in the Lord Jesus Christ has great assurance both in this life and in the next. We live for the Lord in this life, and when our time comes to die, we die for the Lord. He is waiting to receive us into His presence, for we belong to Him. This is a clear promise that the end of this life does not mean extinction but continued life in His presence in the next. He is Lord of all and gives assurance to His people that He will care for them wherever they are. Let us indeed live for Him.

———————————————

Golden thought: **"Whether we live . . . or die, we are the Lord's."** "For to this end Christ both died, and rose, and revived, that he might be Lord both of the dead and living" (Rom. 14:9).

June 16

"*T*hen we which are alive and remain shall be caught up together with them in the clouds to meet the Lord in the air: and so shall we ever be with the Lord" (I Thess. 4:17). The church age will end with the coming of the Lord for His people. He shall call them up into His presence that they might be with Him forever. But He will also resurrect the bodies of all the dead who died in faith in Him. He has a grand purpose for them throughout eternity. They shall serve Him in glory and resurrection power for endless ages. His plans include a new heaven and a new earth in which His people can serve Him forever (Rev. 21:1–3). Let us keep the upward look, watching for His appearing.

Golden thought: **We shall always be with the Lord.**

"Wherefore comfort one another with these words" (I Thess. 4:18).

June 17

"*B*ehold, I shew you a mystery; We shall not all sleep, but we shall all be changed" (I Cor. 15:51). Not every believer will die. In the last generation, believers will be caught up into the presence of the Lord directly. But all believers will have glorious resurrection bodies (I Cor. 15:49). "But now is Christ risen from the dead, and become the firstfruits of them that slept" (I Cor. 15:20). Because He lives in resurrection power, all believers have the assurance that Christ will give them resurrection bodies at the right time. "Flesh and blood cannot inherit the kingdom of God" (I Cor. 15:50). But God has a marvelous purpose for all believers in the ages to come. Praise God for eternal life!

Golden thought: **"We shall all be changed."**

"Therefore, my beloved brethren, be ye stedfast, unmoveable, always abounding in the work of the Lord, forasmuch as ye know that your labour is not in vain in the Lord" (I Cor. 15:58).

June 18

"*A*nd the very God of peace sanctify you wholly; and I pray God your whole spirit and soul and body be preserved blameless unto the coming of our Lord Jesus Christ. Faithful is he that calleth you, who also will do it" (I Thess. 5:23–24). God will certainly answer Paul's prayer for all believers. God intends to set apart all believers for Himself. He will impart to every believer the righteousness of Christ. He is faithful and will preserve them unto His glorious kingdom. Every believer should live with the glorious expectation of living with the Lord throughout endless ages of triumphant service for Him. We may rest assured in His solemn promises.

_____

Golden thought: **Faithful is He who calls you, who also will do it.**

"In every thing give thanks: for this is the will of God in Christ Jesus concerning you" (I Thess. 5:18).

June 19

"*T*hey that trust in the Lord shall be as mount Zion, which cannot be removed, but abideth for ever" (Ps. 125:1). God will uphold His people who trust in Him. His grace and power are much stronger than any mountain. Those who trust in God are planting their lives upon His solemn promise. They shall never be disappointed. In the endless ages to come God will always remember His promises and will keep them to every believer. He has prepared more for them than they can possibly imagine. "Trust in him at all times; ye people, pour out your heart before him: God is a refuge for us" (Ps. 62:8). You can never go wrong by taking God at His word.

Golden thought: **They who trust in the Lord shall be as Mount Zion.**

"I will praise thee, O Lord, with my whole heart" (Ps. 9:1).

June 20

"As the mountains are round about Jerusalem, so the Lord is round about his people from henceforth even for ever" (Ps. 125:2). God is always the real protection for His people. That is why the psalmist claimed Him as "my refuge and my fortress" (Ps. 91:2). In any trouble, we may flee to Him for our defense. David encouraged himself in the Lord: "Though I walk in the midst of trouble, thou wilt revive me" (Ps. 138:7). We need that same confidence in the keeping power of God in our lives. The Lord is with His people every step of their pathway. God will never forsake those He loves. The believer should walk his pathway with serene confidence in the loving care of God.

Golden thought: **The Lord is round about His people forever.**

"Except the Lord build the house, they labour in vain that build it" (Ps. 127:1).

June 21

"*A*nd thine ears shall hear a word behind thee, saying, This is the way, walk ye in it, when ye turn to the right hand, and when ye turn to the left" (Isa. 30:21). God gives guidance to His people. God regularly guides His people through His Word, the Bible. Reading and meditating upon Scripture is the chief way that believers learn God's will. Yet there are times when God lays a direction on the heart of the believer. There are times the believer will get an idea that he should speak to a certain person about the Lord. or that he should write a letter to a friend, telling him about God's blessings. Such ideas should not be shrugged off as "a nice thought." There are times the Lord gives direct leading.

Golden thought: **"This is the way, walk ye in it."**

"Lead me in thy truth, and teach me: for thou art the God of my salvation" (Ps. 25:5).

June 22

"Wherefore he is able also to save them to the uttermost that come unto God by him, seeing he ever liveth to make intercession for them" (Heb. 7:25). The Lord Jesus Christ is the great High Priest of His people. Earthly priests have frailties, but He is able to intercede perfectly for them because He knows them and His Father's will for them perfectly. He has the power to save them from their sins. His Spirit can guide their steps into His path for their lives. No believer should think that his situation is beyond the help of the Lord. No sinner should think that Christ cannot save him. The Lord has all authority in heaven and earth (Matt. 28:18). He is mighty to save.

Golden thought: **"He is able to save them to the uttermost that come unto God by him."**

"For Christ is not entered into the holy places made with hands . . . but into heaven itself, now to appear in the presence of God for us" (Heb. 9:24).

June 23

"*F*or this is good and acceptable in the sight of God our Savior; who will have all men to be saved, and to come to the knowledge of the truth" (I Tim. 2:3–4). God desires all men to be saved and to submit to His Word. He has good will toward all, but all will not be saved because of their sinfulness. God's people are commanded to make prayers and intercessions for all men because some of them will be saved by the grace of God (v. 1). God takes no pleasure in the death of the wicked because He desires all men to be reconciled to Himself. But God is just and will send the wicked to hell in their stubborn resistance. Let us remember to pray for the lost that they might get right with God while there is yet time.

———————————————

Golden thought: **God desires all men to be saved.**

"The Lord . . . is longsuffering to us-ward, not willing that any should perish, but that all should come to repentance" (II Pet. 3:9).

June 24

"For bodily exercise profiteth little: but godliness is profitable unto all things, having promise of the life that now is, and of that which is to come" (I Tim.4:8). Exercise can help some people regain their strength, but godliness is beneficial to every person who seeks God. It is not only a blessing in the present life but it is also the portion of every saint in glory. True godliness comes from the study of God's Word. Paul urged Timothy to give attention to the reading of Scripture and to its teaching (v. 13). The Lord Jesus commanded men to "search the scriptures" (John 5:39). The wholesome teaching of Scripture should shine out through the godly life of every true believer.

Golden thought: **"Godliness is profitable unto all things."**
"Yea, and all that will live godly in Christ Jesus shall suffer persecution" (II Tim. 3:12).

June 25

"*I*t is a faithful saying: For if we be dead with him, we shall also live with him: if we suffer, we shall also reign with him: if we deny him, he also will deny us" (II Tim. 2:11–12). The believer is called upon to die to self, to die to his personal preferences. But if he does, he lives with Christ in service and holiness. If we have to suffer in this world, we shall one day reign with Christ over all. But if we deny Him, He will deny us. He will repudiate the poor testimony that we have been. The believer must focus his attention on the Lord and His testimony. If we please Him, we have won the victory. If we fail Him, we have lost everything. Outward circumstances in this world count for nothing. Jesus is everything.

_____

Golden thought: **"We shall also reign with him."**
"Thou therefore endure hardness, as a good soldier of Jesus Christ" (II Tim. 2:3).

June 26

"*H*enceforth there is laid up for me a crown of righteousness, which the Lord, the righteous judge, shall give me at that day: and not to me only, but unto all them also that love his appearing" (II Tim. 4:8). Paul had labored in preaching the Word, spreading the gospel throughout the known world. Many of his enemies had slandered him, but the Lord promised a crown of righteousness. All believers can take comfort from Paul's example. We too need to be faithful in getting the gospel out and living for the Lord Jesus in this wicked world. He has a crown waiting for everyone who loves the thought of His appearing. Let us continue serving Him with single-minded devotion.

Golden thought: **"There is laid up for me a crown."**

"Yea, and all that will live godly in Christ Jesus shall suffer persecution" (II Tim. 3:12).

June 27

"For God shall bring every work into judgment, with every secret thing, whether it be good, or whether it be evil" (Eccles. 12:14). God will judge the deeds of every last human being. By the grace of the Lord Jesus Christ the believer will have the record of his sins blotted out (Acts 3:19). God the Father will reward his good deeds openly (Matt. 6:4). But God will also repay those who hate Him to their face (Deut. 7:10). He is indeed the Judge of all the earth, who will do right (Gen. 18:25). Every person on earth should order his life so as to be pleasing and obedient to God. But few people have as their purpose the glory of the God of heaven.

Golden thought: **"God shall bring every work into judgment."** "By faith Enoch . . . pleased God" (Heb. 11:5).

June 28

"*B*ut without faith it is impossible to please him: for he that cometh to God must believe that he is, and that he is a rewarder of them that diligently seek him" (Heb. 11:6). The ancient heroes of the faith all demonstrated that they lived for the glory of God alone. The place of the believer is to be diligently seeking God. To please Him should be the highest goal of every believer. By faith the believer should search the Scriptures to find those things that please God and then practice them. Most of mankind live just to please themselves, but the believer should have much higher goals. For all eternity we should be to the praise of His glory.

Golden thought: **He who comes to God must believe that He is and that He is a Rewarder.**

"Now faith is the substance of things hoped for, the evidence of things not seen" (Heb. 11:1).

June 29

"*F*ear not, little flock; for it is your Father's good pleasure to give you the kingdom" (Luke 12:32). Believers should not be troubled by the loss of material goods and worldly pleasures. They may be a small and despised minority here in this world, but in God's coming kingdom they will be the rulers. We should have our hearts set upon that glorious kingdom of God that is yet to come rather than the paltry baubles of the present world system. Our little flock should live to the glory of God and turn our back on the glittering world. We should think of providing treasures for ourselves in the world to come. Let us serve Him in single-minded devotion.

Golden thought: **"It is your Father's good pleasure to give you the kingdom."**

"For where your treasure is, there will your heart be also" (Luke 12:34).

June 30

"For whoso findeth me findeth life, and shall obtain favour of the Lord" (Prov. 8:35). Solomon personifies wisdom as a wise woman calling to people to walk in ways that please God. True wisdom is the fear of the Lord (Prov. 8:13). It is the reverence that puts God first in the life and subordinates all else. Reverence for God means hating evil, pride, and arrogancy (Prov. 8:13). The fruit of wisdom is better than gold (Prov. 8:19). Wisdom can well say, "Blessed is the man that heareth me" (Prov. 8:34). "Happy is the man that findeth wisdom" (Prov. 3:13). "The fear of the Lord is the beginning of wisdom" (Ps. 111:10). "Christ, the power of God, and the wisdom of God" (I Cor. 1:24).

Golden thought: **He who finds wisdom finds life.**

"We speak the wisdom of God in a mystery" (I Cor. 2:7).

July 1

"*O* bless our God, ye people, and make the voice of his praise to be heard: which holdeth our soul in life, and suffereth not our feet to be moved" (Ps. 66:8–9). God's people should praise Him for His lovingkindness and providential care. People do not stay alive just because they eat a balanced diet and take their medicines. God sustains His people and all the earth by His grace. He provides special protection for His people. They are objects of His love. We should remember to praise Him for all His loving care for His people. We should have a serene confidence in God's gracious provisions for His people. He will never forsake His own.

Golden thought: **He does not suffer our feet to be moved.**
"Come and hear, all ye that fear God, and I will declare what he hath done for my soul" (Ps. 66:16).

July 2

"Thou wilt shew me the path of life: in thy presence is fulness of joy; at thy right hand there are pleasures for evermore" (Ps. 16:11). God does not leave His people to stumble in darkness; He guides us homeward to His presence. He shines the light of His Word upon our steps that we may walk safely by His grace. He strengthens us for the journey and guides us by His Word. It is always His purpose to bring His people safely into His presence. He is preparing a blessed place for His people. There we will find everlasting joy in fellowship with Him and with His redeemed people. Our steps should quicken and our heart should leap with joy at the thought of seeing Him face to face.

Golden thought: **"Thou wilt show me the path of life."**
"Hold up my goings in thy paths, that my footsteps slip not" (Ps. 17:5).

July 3

"*T*he meek will he guide in judgment: and the meek will he teach his way" (Ps. 25:9). People who desire to obey God will find that He leads them through His Word. They will find that all the paths of the Lord are mercy and truth to the obedient souls (Ps. 25:10). No man is clever enough to avoid all the pitfalls of life, but the Lord can guide His people safely through them all. But there must be an attitude of meek submission to the will of the Lord. Those who run ahead of the Lord will stumble and fall, but those who follow Him in obedience will find that His way is perfect. He can guide us safely past every snare and stumbling block. Let us trust Him every step of the way.

Golden thought: **"The meek will he teach his way."**
"All the paths of the Lord are mercy and truth unto such as keep his covenant and his testimonies" (Ps. 25:10).

July 4

"*If* the Son therefore shall make you free, ye shall be free indeed" (John 8:36). Freedom is a precious gift, but most of the people who think they are free are really slaves to their own sins and passions. But if they will come to the Lord Jesus Christ, He will break their chains and set them free to serve God as they desire. Freedom comes to those who search the Scriptures and learn what the will of God is for their lives. Obedience to God's Word makes a person free to accomplish the noble desires of his heart. The freedom that God imparts enables a person to do the will of God in all his ways and in any circumstances. That person is free because he is a servant of God.

Golden thought: **You shall be free indeed.**

Jesus said, "Whosoever committeth sin is the servant of sin" (John 8:34).

July 5

"*B*eloved, now are we the sons of God, and it doth not yet appear what we shall be: but we know that, when he shall appear, we shall be like him; for we shall see him as he is" (I John 3:2). Those who have received the Lord Jesus Christ as their personal Savior are made children of God by His grace. We are yet far from home, but when He comes again in glory, He shall call up His children into His presence. We shall be like Him in a glorious resurrection body, "for we shall see him as he is." He now shines in splendor in the presence of His heavenly Father. By His promise we shall abide in that glory with Him forever and ever. "Every man that hath this hope in him purifieth himself, even as he is pure" (I John 3:3).

Golden thought: **We shall be like Him.**

"Behold, what manner of love the Father hath bestowed upon us, that we should be called the sons of God" (I John 3:1).

July 6

"*I*n this was manifested the love of God toward us, because that God sent his only begotten Son into the world, that we might live through him" (I John 4:9). The Lord Jesus Christ, God's Son, came into the world to die for the sins of mankind. His sacrifice upon the cross was the atonement for our sins. God promises life eternal to all who will trust Christ for their salvation. Christ is the Savior of all who will believe in Him. No one can atone for his own sins, but Christ's death is the once-for-all sacrifice for sin. It was infinite love that caused Christ to die for us. Let us receive that gift with humble thanksgiving and rest upon His promised salvation.

Golden thought: **God sent His Son into the world that we might live through Him.**

"Herein is love, not that we loved God, but that he loved us, and sent his Son to be the propitiation for our sins" (I John 4:10).

July 7

"*B*ut God will redeem my soul from the power of the grave: for he shall receive me" (Ps. 49:15). The death of the Redeemer, Jesus Christ, is the sacrifice that sets us free from sin and the grave. We may come to God in simple faith in the Lord Jesus and be sure that God will receive us for Jesus' sake. His death on the cross paid the price for all our sins. People who die in their sins will carry nothing away from this world but the guilt of their sins (Ps. 49:17). Those who know the Lord Jesus as Savior will share the faith of the psalmist. "Whosoever shall call upon the name of the Lord shall be saved" (Rom. 10:13). Call upon Him and receive His promise.

Golden thought: **"God will redeem my soul from the power of the grave."**

"And the heavens shall declare his righteousness: for God is judge himself" (Ps. 50:6).

July 8

"And call upon me in the day of trouble: I will deliver thee, and thou shalt glorify me" (Ps. 50:15). God invites His people to call upon Him in prayer for any trouble at any time. He is prepared to help His people no matter what the circumstances are. God can help His people by giving them eternal life or by supplying daily bread. God's people need to get into the habit of praying to God for help in every time of need. The wicked have no such access to God (Ps. 50:16). But God loves to hear from His people and rejoices to supply to them the help they need. Every time of trouble is an opportunity to talk to the Lord and to get to know Him in a deeper way.

Golden thought: **"I will deliver thee, and thou shalt glorify me."**
"Hear my prayer, O God; give ear to the words of my mouth" (Ps. 54:2).

July 9

"*I* say unto you, that likewise joy shall be in heaven over one sinner that repenteth, more than over ninety and nine just persons, which need no repentance" (Luke 15:7). God rejoices over the conversion of a dark-dyed sinner more than over religious people who are not conscious of their need. God listens to the prayers of all, but He treasures the cry of the sinner for salvation. He is ready to hear the prodigal and to forgive. The Pharisees needed the forgiveness of God as much as the prodigal did, but they would not ask. We need to come boldly by the merits of Jesus Christ to ask for God's forgiveness. He rejoices to cleanse away every stain.

Golden thought: **Joy shall be in heaven over one sinner who repents.**

"But the end of all things is at hand: be ye therefore sober, and watch unto prayer" (I Pet. 4:7).

July 10

"*He* that hath an ear, let him hear what the Spirit saith unto the churches; to him that overcometh will I give to eat of the tree of life, which is in the midst of the paradise of God" (Rev. 2:7). The overcomer is the true believer in the Lord Jesus Christ. The Lord promises him the right to eat of the tree of life. The tree disappeared from the face of the earth, but it is now in heaven. Heaven should not be thought of as an abstract realm with no beauty. The lovely gardens of earth are a mere foretaste of the beautiful paradise of God that He has prepared for His people (Rev. 22:1–2). No good thing will He withhold from His redeemed saints.

Golden thought: **To the overcomer God will give to eat of the tree of life.**

"Blessed is he that keepeth the sayings of the prophecy of this book" (Rev. 22:7).

July 11

"He that overcometh shall not be hurt of the second death" (Rev. 2:11). The overcomer, the true believer, cannot be hurt by the second death because he has passed from death unto life in Christ Jesus. If the Lord tarry, he may pass through physical death into the presence of the Lord, but he cannot die eternally because Christ has made him alive. "For the wages of sin is death; but the gift of God is eternal life through Jesus Christ our Lord" (Rom. 6:23). Because He lives, we shall live also. "For the law of the Spirit of life in Christ Jesus hath made me free from the law of sin and death" (Rom. 8:2). Believers can praise God for eternal deliverance from death by the grace of the Lord Jesus Christ.

Golden thought: **The overcomer shall not be hurt by the second death.**

"But put ye on the Lord Jesus Christ, and make not provision for the flesh, to fulfil the lusts thereof" (Rom. 13:14).

July 12

"*T*o him that overcometh will I give to eat of the hidden manna, and will give him a white stone, and in the stone a new name written, which no man knoweth saving he that receiveth it" (Rev. 2:17). The Lord Jesus gives to the overcomer, the true believer, permission to eat the heavenly manna. The manna in the wilderness sustained the Israelites for forty years, but God's hidden manna provides constant spiritual strength to the believer all his life. The white stone was the vote of approval in the ancient world. This is so specific that the believer's heavenly name is inscribed upon the stone. The believer may well ponder what will be his new name in glory.

Golden thought: **Christ gives inner strength and a vote of confidence to the believer.**

"Sing aloud unto God our strength: make a joyful noise unto the God of Jacob" (Ps. 81:1).

July 13

*A*nd he that overcometh, and keepeth my works unto the end, to him will I give power over the nations. . . . And I will give him the morning star" (Rev. 2:26, 28). The Lord promises to the overcomer, the true believer, that He will give him authority over the nations in the world to come. The Lord has a grand purpose for believers. But He also promises believers that He will give them the morning star, a title that the Lord Himself claims (Rev. 22:16). Thus, the Lord is promising that He will give Himself to His people. He not only died to save them but He also gives Himself to them in eternal love. How infinite is His love! How great should be the love that believers have for Him!

Golden thought: **Jesus says, "I will give him the morning star."** Paul prays that believers would "know the love of Christ, which passeth knowledge" (Eph. 3:19).

July 14

"*F*or with thee is the fountain of life: in thy light shall we see light" (Ps. 36:9). God pours life into the believer like a fountain. But He is not only the water of life for the believer; He is also the Light of his life. We can see the light only as God illuminates us with His light. The Lord Jesus claimed, "As long as I am in the world, I am the light of the world" (John 9:5). We see in the love of God and the compassion of the Lord Jesus light that transforms mankind. We should let that light shine through us that the world may see Jesus in us. The believer should let the light shine through him that the Lord might illuminate the darkness around him.

Golden thought: **"In thy light shall we see light."**
"For ye were sometimes darkness, but now are ye light in the Lord: walk as children of light" (Eph. 5:8).

July 15

"*I*n my Father's house are many mansions: if it were not so, I would have told you. I go to prepare a place for you" (John 14:2). The Lord Jesus assured His people that His Father has made adequate provision for His people in the life beyond this world. He will go to prepare a suitable place for His followers to dwell in for all eternity. This world is merely His footstool; the next is His throne room. God's people may rest assured that the place He prepares for them will be beautiful and satisfying beyond anything we can imagine. We must not allow our hearts to be troubled by adversity in this life. In the next realm we shall be satisfied and astonished by what He has prepared for His people.

Golden thought: **Jesus said, "I go to prepare a place for you."** "And the Spirit and the bride say, Come. And let him that heareth say, Come" (Rev. 22:17).

July 16

"*A*nd if I go and prepare a place for you, I will come again, and receive you unto myself; that where I am, there ye may be also" (John 14:3). The Lord Jesus will not only prepare heaven for His people, but He will also return to escort His people to that glorious place. The Second Coming in glory is clearly taught in Scripture. All His believers may rest assured that the Lord Jesus will come again and will fulfill all His promises to His people. The eternal fellowship with God will be a joy and satisfaction to all the people of God. Their surroundings will be appropriate for the eternal celebration of the greatness and love of God. By then they will know that He has done all things well.

Golden thought: **Jesus said, "I will come again, and receive you unto myself."**

"Whither I go, thou canst not follow me now; but thou shalt follow me afterwards" (John 13:36).

July 17

"Jesus saith unto him, I am the way, the truth, and the life: no man cometh unto the Father, but by me" (John 14:6). Trust in the Lord Jesus is the way to God. His person is the truth about the meaning of life. Faith in Him means life everlasting for His people. Through the Lord Jesus, His people come to God as their heavenly Father, who loves and cares for them. Apart from the Lord Jesus all men are lost in sin. But a loving God sent His Son into the world to redeem men and prepare them for eternal joy and service in heaven. Believers need to get the gospel message out so that others may hear and come to the Savior that they might have eternal life in Him.

Golden thought: **Jesus said, "I am the way, the truth, and the life."** Jesus said, "Believe me that I am in the Father, and the Father in me" (John 14:11).

July 18

"And whatsoever ye shall ask in my name, that will I do, that the Father may be glorified in the Son" (John 14:13). Now believers pray in the name of Jesus, that He may accomplish His Father's will in us. The Father is pleased that men honor His Son. We should ask in faith, believing that He will indeed answer our prayers. But we must also take heed that we pray according to His will and not just for vain trinkets and pleasures. Few Christians pray for wisdom and boldness in testimony. But God is pleased to hear and answer the earnest prayers of His people. We must leave the timing of the answer in His hands. We are usually in a hurry, but God is always right on time in His answers. Trust Him.

_____

Golden thought: **Whatever you ask in Jesus' name, He will do.**

"If ye love me, keep my commandments" (John 14:15).

July 19

"*A*nd I will pray the Father, and he shall give you another Comforter, that he may abide with you for ever" (John 14:16). This is the promise of the gift of the Holy Spirit in the heart of every believer. The initial fulfillment came on the day of Pentecost (Acts 2). From the day of Pentecost on, the Spirit of God dwells within the hearts of His people. He is called actively *the Comforter* because He brings comfort and consolation to His people. He is one called alongside to help the believer in time of need. He provides encouragement, strength, guidance, and wisdom that the believer needs. Every believer should submit to His leading and should serve God through the strength of the Spirit.

───────────────

Golden thought: **God shall give you another Comforter.**
"For as many as are led by the Spirit of God, they are the sons of God" (Rom. 8:14).

July 20

"*B*ut the Comforter, which is the Holy Ghost, whom the Father will send in my name, he shall teach you all things, and bring all things to your remembrance, whatsoever I have said unto you" (John 14:26). Part of the ministry of the Spirit is to impart wisdom and understanding to the believer. He causes the saints to remember the portions of Scripture they need for edification and testimony to others. The believer should witness for Christ, not by argument but by allowing the Spirit to bring verses to bear on the person's heart. The Spirit alone can convict of sin. All believers should follow the leading of the Spirit in their daily walk with God.

Golden thought: **The Comforter shall teach you all things.**
"Quench not the Spirit" (I Thess. 5:19).

July 21

"Through God we shall do valiantly: for he it is that shall tread down our enemies" (Ps. 60:12). God sustains and delivers His people. Through His power God's people triumph. Our enemies may outnumber us, but God can still deal with all of them. The Devil and his helpers may attack us. Through God's power the saints can overcome any foes. We must not count on our strength and steadfastness. We can easily fail, but God will never fail His people. Through God we can serve acceptably; through God we can conquer the old, evil foe; through God we can defeat the Devil and all his demonic henchmen. Let us trust Him to do it.

Golden thought: **"Through God we shall do valiantly."**
"But I will sing of thy power; yea, I will sing aloud of thy mercy in the morning" (Ps. 59:16).

July 22

"Then shalt thou call, and the Lord shall answer; thou shalt cry, and he shall say, Here I am" (Isa. 58:9). When God's people please the Lord, His answers to their prayers are speedy. When they forget about His will, the answers are delayed. We all need to keep in daily fellowship with the Lord and to seek to please Him at all times. The closer we walk with the Lord, the better our prayer life becomes. But sometimes there are prayers that He cannot answer because we are not ready for the answer. We need to prepare our hearts and to seek His face that we may be ready for His gracious answer. Let us seek Him diligently.

Golden thought: **"Thou shalt cry, and he shall say, Here I am."** "Hear my prayer, O Lord, and let my cry come unto thee" (Ps. 102:1).

July 23

"And if thou draw out thy soul to the hungry, and satisfy the afflicted soul; then shall thy light rise in obscurity, and thy darkness be as the noon day" (Isa. 58:10). When God's people take seriously the plight of the poor and afflicted, God is highly pleased. Since He pays special attention to them, His people ought to be aware of their needs as well. The Lord is pleased to bless the people who care for the unfortunate. The Lord said to the rich young ruler, "give to the poor, and thou shalt have treasure in heaven" (Mark 10:21). People will remember the generous deeds done to them, and the Lord will remember also.

Golden thought: **If you satisfy the afflicted soul, your light shall rise.**

"Only they would that we should remember the poor; the same which I also was forward to do" (Gal. 2:10).

July 24

"And thine house and thy kingdom shall be established for ever before thee: thy throne shall be established for ever. According to all these words, and according to all this vision, so did Nathan speak unto David" (II Sam. 7:16–17). Nathan's prophecy to David revealed the Davidic covenant that God had promised to David. It will ultimately be fulfilled in the future reign of the Lord Jesus Christ (Matt. 1:1; Luke 1:31–33). The Lord Jesus testified of this as well in the book of Revelation (3:7; 22:16). The Lord's kingdom will be universal and will never end. But it awaits the coming of the Lord, who alone can establish the kingdom.

Golden thought: **"Thy kingdom shall be established for ever before thee."**

"For the Son of man shall come in the glory of his Father with his angels; and then he shall reward every man according to his works" (Matt. 16:27).

July 25

"*B*lessed is he that considereth the poor: the Lord will deliver him in time of trouble" (Ps. 41:1). The Lord observes how a person treats the poor. If he is compassionate towards them, the Lord will deliver him in the time of his trouble. The Lord will bring blessing upon the compassionate (v. 2). We should all be sensitive to the plight of the unfortunate. We have needs ourselves and trust that the Lord will provide for us. The Lord Jesus left us an example of how He went out of His way to meet the needs of the poor and the suffering. Believers ought to manifest a similar spirit of compassion to those in need.

Golden thought: **"The Lord will deliver him in time of trouble."**
"The Lord will preserve him, and keep him alive; and he shall be blessed upon the earth" (Ps. 41:2).

July 26

"My flesh and my heart faileth: but God is the strength of my heart, and my portion for ever" (Ps. 73:26). Circumstances may cause the believer to panic, but he should always remember God. There may be no encouraging help in sight in this world, but always God is the strength of His people. The believer has inner resources of divine strength and grace. God can sustain him in any extremity. But the psalmist claims God as his portion forever. The believer may claim God as his protection and source of help throughout the ages. God will never forsake His people. His loving care rests upon them forever. Let us walk in faith, resting upon His sure promise.

Golden thought: **God is my portion forever.**

"It is good for me to draw near to God: I have put my trust in the Lord God" (Ps. 73:28).

July 27

"*I* am the Lord thy God, which brought thee out of the land of Egypt: open thy mouth wide, and I will fill it" (Ps. 81:10). God promised the Israelites abundant blessings, but they did not listen to His Word. They walked in their own counsels. He invited them to open their mouths like baby birds, and He would fill them. But they turned to their own resources. We should not err as they did. We need to open our mouths for the blessings and answers to prayer that God is ready to pour out upon His people. We need to come before His presence to ask Him for grace and strength to live for Him each day. Let us trust Him for answers greater than our requests.

Golden thought: **"Open thy mouth wide, and I will fill it."**
"With honey out of the rock should I have satisfied thee" (Ps. 81:16).

July 28

"So Christ was once offered to bear the sins of many; and unto them that look for him shall he appear the second time without sin unto salvation" (Heb. 9:28). All those who look for the Lord Jesus Christ for salvation will find that He is the Almighty Savior who can deliver them from sin. He offered Himself upon the cross for the sins of the world. Whoever trusts in Him for salvation is assured that He will cleanse every stain. At His second advent He will remove even the presence of sin in the glorious kingdom reign that He will bring. His goal for every believer is freedom from sin and the attainment of absolute perfection in the holiness of God. Even so, come Lord Jesus.

Golden thought: **Unto them who look for Him unto salvation shall He appear without sin.**

Jesus is "called of God an high priest after the order of Melchizedek" (Heb. 5:10).

July 29

"*This* is the covenant that I will make with them after those days, saith the Lord, I will put my laws into their hearts, and in their minds will I write them; and their sins and iniquities will I remember no more" (Heb. 10:16–17). The new covenant in Christ does not depend on outward rituals but on a heart relationship with Him. The Lord puts His Word into the hearts and minds of His people and directs their paths through the Scriptures. Their sins are under His blood of Calvary. Now He leads His people ever closer to His Father. When we walk according to His Word, we draw ever closer to His heavenly Father. Let us press forward on the upper way.

Golden thought: **"I will put my laws into their hearts, and in their minds will I write them."**

"Cast not away therefore your confidence, which hath great recompense of reward" (Heb. 10:35).

July 30

"And it shall come to pass in the last days, that the mountain of the Lord's house shall be established in the top of the mountains, and shall be exalted above the hills; and all nations shall flow unto it" (Isa. 2:2). The word *mountain* is often used as a symbol of a kingdom. The kingdom of the Lord will one day be exalted over all human kingdoms. The book of Revelation describes a great kingdom reign on earth and then a glorious eternal reign (Rev. 20:4; 21:1–4). In spite of the proud reign of sin in the present world system, believers look forward to that time in which the Lord will bring all into subjection to His will. "The earth is the Lord's" (Ps. 24:1), and He shall yet rule it perfectly.

Golden thought: **The Lord's kingdom shall yet be established over all.**

"Lift up your heads, O ye gates . . . and the King of glory shall come in" (Ps. 24:9).

July 31

"*For* with God nothing shall be impossible" (Luke 1:37). The angel Gabriel spoke these words to Mary after imparting to her the prophecy of the Virgin Birth, which would soon take place. Mary believed the angel and gave herself to the Lord's service. All believers need to share her serene trust in God. In spite of great difficulties, she never wavered in her obedience. God intends to work marvelous deeds for His people. He will transform them into powerful saints for Him. We should never be skeptical of the Lord's ability to perform what He has promised. In His infinite wisdom He knows just how and when to work His will on earth. We need to follow His Word with trust and submission.

Golden thought: **"With God nothing shall be impossible."**
"Now our Lord Jesus Christ . . . stablish you in every good word and work" (II Thess. 2:16–17).

August 1

"There shall come a Star out of Jacob, and a Sceptre shall rise out of Israel, and shall smite the corners of Moab, and destroy all the children of Sheth" (Num. 24:17). The *Star* is a symbol for the Messiah, the Lord Jesus Christ. The Lord claimed to be "the bright and morning star" (Rev. 22:16). He will "destroy all the children of Sheth [tumult]" When the Lord comes in glory, He will destroy the wicked from His kingdom. He will then bring in the great reign of peace on earth and good will toward men (Luke 2:14). He alone will rule the world in peace and righteousness. He is "the Prince of Peace" (Isa. 9:6), and "The Lord our Righteousness" (Jer. 23:6).

Golden thought: **"There shall come a Star out of Jacob."**

"Lift up your heads, O ye gates; even lift them up, ye everlasting doors; and the King of glory shall come in" (Ps. 24:9).

August 2

"For unto us a child is born, unto us a son is given: and the government shall be upon his shoulder: and his name shall be called Wonder of a Counsellor, God of Might, Father of Eternity, Prince of Peace" (Isa. 9:6, author's translation). Isaiah prophesies the birth of the Lord Jesus Christ, the Son of God, and gives Him titles appropriate for His glorious position. The Lord alone has the power and wisdom to rule all things perfectly. He was born in a lowly state at Bethlehem (and the angels sang), but the day will come when He shall reign in glory and power (and the angels will hasten to do His bidding). Let us be zealous to do His bidding now and to please Him.

Golden thought: **"Unto us a child is born, unto us a son is given."** "Of the increase of his government and peace there shall be no end" (Isa. 9:7).

August 3

"And there shall come forth a rod out of the stem of Jesse, and a Branch shall grow out of his roots" (Isa. 11:1). The messianic line shall produce a mighty King, the Lord Jesus Christ. At the triumphal entry the multitudes hailed Him as "the Son of David" (Matt. 21:9). The Spirit of the Lord shall rest upon Him (Isa. 11:2). He is the only one who can judge the poor with righteousness (Isa. 11:4). The Lord Jesus claims, "I am the root and the offspring of David" (Rev. 22:16). When He reigns, "the earth shall be full of the knowledge of the Lord, as the waters cover the sea" (Isa. 11:9). Let us obey Him now and do those things that are pleasing in His sight.

Golden thought: **A rod shall come forth from the stem of Jesse.**
"The Lord Jehovah is my strength and my song; he also is become my salvation" (Isa. 12:2).

August 4

"And whosoever shall give to drink onto one of these little ones a cup of cold water only in the name of a disciple, verily I say unto you, he shall in no wise lose his reward" (Matt. 10:42). God rewards not only great deeds done for Him but also the simplest kindnesses done in His name. A cup of cold water does not cost much, but it can be refreshing to those who are tired and thirsty. We should not miss opportunities to help others just because they are minor deeds. Believers can oftentimes serve Christ well in their everyday activities if they will just keep their eyes open for opportunities. To be known as a follower of Christ who thinks of others and seeks to help where he can is a clear testimony for Him.

_____

Golden thought: **"He shall in no wise lose his reward."**

"For ye were sometimes darkness, but now are ye light in the Lord: walk as children of light" (Eph. 5:8).

August 5

"And whatsoever ye do, do it heartily, as to the Lord, and not unto men; knowing that of the Lord ye shall receive the reward of the inheritance: for ye serve the Lord Christ" (Col. 3:23–24). Every good thing the believer tries to do, he should do for the Lord and His glory. To try to please men is a hopeless task, but the Lord delights in those who seek to please Him. We should serve Him with zeal and enthusiasm. The reward is His approval, which alone is enough. But He also promises the reward of a vast inheritance in the world to come. He delights in blessing His people in this life and in the life to come. How can we not serve Him above all things!

_____

Golden thought: **"Ye shall receive the reward of the inheritance."**
The Lord said, "Fear not, Abram: I am thy shield, and thy exceeding great reward" (Gen. 15:1).

August 6

"Many shall be purified, and made white, and tried; but the wicked shall do wickedly: and none of the wicked shall understand; but the wise shall understand" (Dan. 12:10). Daniel prophesies of the future that God will purify many of His saints, but the wicked will continue on in their sins. Sinful people do not understand the Word and will of God. But God gives here a wonderful promise: "The wise shall understand." God shall impart wisdom to His people. Christ is "the power of God and the wisdom of God" (I Cor. 1:24). Believers must trust the Lord to supply to them the wisdom they need to live for God in the midst of a wicked generation.

Golden thought: **"The wise shall understand."**

"The wise in heart will receive commandments: but a prating fool shall fall" (Prov. 10:8).

August 7

"Though hand join in hand, the wicked shall not be unpunished: but the seed of the righteous shall be delivered" (Prov. 11:21). Sinners always think that they can somehow get away with sin. Although wicked people may form a wide conspiracy, yet God will punish their evil deeds. No one can get away with sin. But God will deliver His people. There is forgiveness in Christ. "In whom we have redemption through his blood, the forgiveness of sins, according to the riches of his grace" (Eph. 1:7). The person who repents of his sin and asks God for forgiveness in Christ can be sure that God hears his prayer and answers in forgiving grace. Praise God for deliverance from sin.

Golden thought: **"The seed of the righteous shall be delivered."**
"And you hath he quickened, who were dead in trespasses and sins" (Eph. 2:1).

August 8

"For by grace are ye saved through faith; and that not of yourselves: it is the gift of God" (Eph. 2:8). God promises the gift of salvation to everyone who believes in the Lord Jesus Christ for forgiveness. His death upon the cross of Calvary atones for our sins. By the grace of God our sins are blotted out. God will remember them against us no more. Salvation is "not of works, lest any man should boast" (Eph. 2:9). Those who trust Christ for salvation "are no more strangers and foreigners, but fellowcitizens with the saints, and of the household of God" (Eph. 2:19). We should praise God for the greatness of the salvation that is granted to us in Christ Jesus.

Golden thought: **By grace are you saved through faith.**

"But now in Christ Jesus ye who sometimes were far off are made nigh by the blood of Christ" (Eph. 2:13).

August 9

"Above all, taking the shield of faith, wherewith ye shall be able to quench all the fiery darts of the wicked" (Eph. 6:16). Paul draws his illustration from ancient warfare. When the enemy shot flaming arrows at Roman soldiers, they would strike harmlessly against the shields the Roman soldiers carried. In the same way, when the believer walks in faith, the poisonous thoughts from the Devil are held at arms' length by the shield of faith. At times young believers are not aware of such attacks and wonder why their thoughts are so terrified. Believers need to stand their ground against the attacks of the Devil and pray for sustaining grace. We need the whole armor of God (Eph. 6:13).

Golden thought: **You shall be able to quench all the fiery darts of the wicked.**

"Put on the whole armour of God, that ye may be able to stand against the wiles of the devil" (Eph. 6:11).

August 10

"*T*he blessing of the Lord, it maketh rich, and he addeth no sorrow with it" (Prov. 10:22). When God brings His blessing into the believer's life, there are no sorrows connected with it. Worldly riches always bring sorrow and worry to the people who possess them. But God's blessings are wholly beneficial. God's blessings often flow through the believer to touch the lives of many others for good. God can impart spiritual riches that are a lifelong blessing, both to the believer, and to those his life may influence for God. Let us not set our hearts on worldly riches but on the blessing of God, which will never pass away. His riches bring the joy of the Lord.

Golden thought: **The blessing of the Lord makes rich.**

"Blessings are upon the head of the just" (Prov. 10:6).

August 11

"For the wages of sin is death; but the gift of God is eternal life through Jesus Christ our Lord" (Rom. 6:23). "Behold, ye have sinned against the Lord: and be sure your sin will find you out" (Num. 32:23). People who hide their sins fool only themselves. Only God can remove sin from the life. All sin is ultimately against God. He will see to it that your sin comes back to confront you. The elaborate plans of the sinner are all in vain. God records every sin, and either you will face them here and ask for God's forgiveness, or you will face them in the life to come with no hope of forgiveness. Ask the Lord Jesus Christ for the gift of the forgiveness of sins, which brings eternal life.

Golden thought: **"The gift of God is eternal life through Jesus Christ."**

"Let not sin therefore reign in your mortal body" (Rom. 6:12).

August 12

"*If* ye abide in me, and my words abide in you, ye shall ask what ye will, and it shall be done unto you" (John 15:7). To abide in Christ is to continue in loving fellowship with Him. If we continue abiding in Christ and His Word, we will find that we have increased freedom in prayer. We will understand His will and be more careful to pray according to it. God can never answer prayer that is contrary to His will. But God delights in answering prayer that His people make to Him, when they pray scripturally in keeping with His Word. The old saints used to pray using the very wording of Scripture. The closer we can come to the thought of Scripture, the surer the answer will be.

Golden thought: **If you abide in me, you shall ask what you will and it shall be done.**

"Abide in me, and I in you. As the branch cannot bear fruit of itself, except it abide in the vine: no more can ye, except ye abide in me" (John 15:4).

August 13

"*I*f ye keep my commandments, ye shall abide in my love; even as I have kept my Father's commandments, and abide in his love" (John 15:10). The privilege of keeping Christ's commandments results in the wondrous opportunity of abiding in His love. The thought of His infinite love surrounding us constantly is well worth pondering. But then He raises the image to a higher level by saying, "Even as I have kept [perfectly] my Father's commandments, and abide in his love." That must be a perfect abiding in infinite love. He sets before us the highest privilege and opens the door wide. Let us indeed keep His commandments and seek to abide in His perfect love.

Golden thought: **If you keep my commands, you shall abide in my love.**

"These things have I spoken unto you, that my joy might abide in you" (John 15:11, Greek text).

August 14

"*Ye* have not chosen me, but I have chosen you, and ordained you, that ye should go and bring forth fruit, and that your fruit should remain" (John 15:16). The Lord Jesus Christ chose the disciples and ordained them to be His servants in raising up believers who would be His church. The fruit of their ministry would be the nucleus of the church that would follow. Their fruit, the converts, would remain for all eternity. In the same way, every person we lead to the Lord is fruit that will remain. The souls we lead to the Lord will be in glory forever. That thought should stir us up to win others for the Lord that they might be fruit for the Lord in eternity.

Golden thought: **I have chosen you that you should bring forth fruit.**

"The fruit of the righteous is a tree of life; and he that winneth souls is wise" (Prov. 11:30).

August 15

"*B*ut when the Comforter is come, whom I will send unto you from the Father, even the Spirit of truth, which proceedeth from the Father, he shall testify of me: and ye also shall bear witness" (John 15:26–27). The Lord Jesus promises that He will send the Comforter, the Holy Spirit, to His people. The ministry of the Spirit will be to bring others to the Lord Jesus; He shall testify of the saving power of Christ. His ministry will bring comfort, help, and strength to the believer. Each of the three Persons of the Trinity is active in our salvation. "And ye also shall bear witness." It is the place of every believer to bear witness to the Lord Jesus as his Savior that others may hear the gospel and be saved.

Golden thought: **He shall testify of me, and you also shall bear witness.**

"We have seen it, and bear witness, and shew unto you that eternal life, which was with the Father, and was manifest to us" (I John 1:2).

August 16

"*H*is king shall be higher than Agag, and his kingdom shall be exalted" (Num. 24:7). The King of Israel will be a great high King. Balaam here prophesies that the king of Israel shall be higher than Agag, who was king of the Amalekites (I Sam. 15:8). He prophesies that His kingdom shall be exalted. Thus, even those of other nations spoke of the greatness of the Jewish Messiah who was to come. It is not a surprise that, when Jesus was born, the wise men came from other nations to bring tribute to the new-born King (Matt. 2:1–12). The Lord Jesus commanded the disciples to go and make disciples of all nations (Matt. 28:19). That is still our commission.

Golden thought: **"His kingdom shall be exalted."**
"Ye shall be witnesses unto me . . . unto the uttermost part of the earth" (Acts 1:8).

August 17

"*I* will set up thy seed after thee, which shall proceed out of thy bowels, and I will establish his kingdom. He shall build an house for my name, and I will stablish the throne of his kingdom for ever" (II Sam. 7:12–13). God promised David that He would set up Solomon as king after him. He would build the temple, but his kingdom would last long after the temple would be destroyed. This is another messianic prophecy, for the eternal kingdom will be the Lord's. Jesus Christ, son of David, will be the eternal King (Matt. 21:9). Every true believer will be part of that kingdom. "For so an entrance shall be ministered unto you abundantly into the everlasting kingdom of our Lord and Saviour Jesus Christ" (II Pet. 1:11).

Golden thought: **I will establish the throne of His kingdom forever.**

"Walk worthy of God, who hath called you unto his kingdom and glory" (I Thess. 2:12).

August 18

"*For* whosoever shall do the will of God, the same is my brother, and my sister, and mother" (Mark 3:35). The Lord Jesus showed no personal favoritism toward His earthly family members. Every believer who trusts Him for salvation is a member of His family. Obedience to the will of God is far more important than any earthly family relationships. Missionaries often have to leave family and friends behind them, but the Lord Jesus Christ is always with them. All believers should recognize that doing the will of God is more important than anything else in this world. Let us all seek to please and honor the Lord Jesus above all things.

Golden thought: **Jesus said that whoever will do the will of God is His brother and sister.**

"As the servants of Christ, doing the will of God from the heart" (Eph. 6:6).

August 19

"*A*nd he said unto them, Take heed what ye hear: with what measure ye mete, it shall be measured to you: and unto you that hear shall more be given" (Mark 4:24). The Lord Jesus gives a major spiritual principle in these words. If a preacher doles out just a tiny bit of truth in his sermons, that is all he will be able to see. But if he spreads out a spiritual banquet for his people, he will be able to see more and more in Scripture. Any saint who drinks deeply at the spring of spiritual truth in Scripture will be able to see more and more in the Word. Any believer who seeks to obey more of what is in Scripture will see more and more truth in it.

——————————————————

Golden thought: **"Unto you that hear shall more be given."**
"Search the scriptures; for in them ye think ye have eternal life: and they are they which testify of me" (John 5:39).

August 20

"*I*f then God so clothe the grass, which is to day in the field, and to morrow is cast into the oven; how much more will he clothe you, O ye of little faith?" (Luke 12:28). When we think of the fields of spring flowers, we think of their fantastic beauty. But they are soon cut down by the reapers or eaten by animals. If God provides such beauty for such a short time, will He not provide something far better for His people? He will not only provide for them in this world but He also will provide eternal habitations for them in the world to come. But there He will present His people with a place of amazing beauty that shall never fade away (Rev. 21:10–22:3). Let us trust Him for it.

Golden thought: **"How much more will he clothe you?"**
"Blessed is he that keepeth the sayings of the prophecy of this book" (Rev. 22:7).

August 21

"*Yea*, and all that will live godly in Christ Jesus shall suffer persecution" (II Tim. 3:12). This is a sobering promise. There may be some Christians who try to hide in the shrubbery and not be recognized as Christians, but if a believer lives a godly life day by day, the world will notice. There will be some who go out of their way to discredit the believer or to harm his testimony. Open persecution is always a possibility, but we must continue living for Jesus in this wicked world. Sometimes the persecution takes the form of mockery and jeering; at other times real harm is intended. We ought to live for Jesus whatever the cost. The best testimony we can have is to stand true to Him whatever the cost.

———————————————

Golden thought: **All that will live godly in Christ shall suffer persecution.**

"But and if ye suffer for righteousness' sake, happy are ye" (I Pet. 3:14).

August 22

"The Lord is not slack concerning his promise, as some men count slackness; but is longsuffering to us-ward, not willing that any should perish, but that all should come to repentance" (II Pet. 3:9). The Lord will certainly keep His promises, but He often delays because we are not ready for them. Plainly we need to change for the better. Unbelievers need to forsake their sinful ways and come to God for forgiveness. Believers need to put God at the center of their activities and honor Him as they should. If anyone will change, or repent, God is quick to respond according to His many promises. We need to draw closer to God to see His promises fulfilled.

Golden thought: **God desires that all come to repentance.**

"Be diligent that ye may be found of him in peace, without spot, and blameless" (II Pet. 3:14).

August 23

"*H*e that dwelleth in the secret place of the most High shall abide under the shadow of the Almighty" (Ps. 91:1). The believer needs to make a practice of living his life in the presence of God. He needs to be conscious of God in all the busy activities of his day. There is a secret place of fellowship that the believer may remain in whatever the outward circumstances may be. He may silently talk with the Lord in the midst of the confusion of life. In that secret place God becomes a vast sheltering presence, a protection from all harm. He, the Almighty, can certainly guide His servant through all the trials and opportunities of the day. We must remain in that secret place of His presence.

Golden thought: **He shall abide under the shadow of the Almighty.**

"And let the beauty of the Lord our God be upon us: and establish thou the work of our hands upon us" (Ps. 90:17).

August 24

"Surely he shall deliver thee from the snare of the fowler, and from the noisome pestilence" (Ps. 91:3). We cannot know the many traps that await us. Unknown enemies and the Devil himself lay clever snares for us. But the Lord sees every snare and can give us grace and guidance to avoid them all. Dreadful disease may stalk the land, but God can protect His people. Every believer must cultivate the attitude of serene trust in the keeping power of God. Although we are traveling through enemy territory, God intends to bring us safely home to His place that He is preparing for His people. We may be confident that the Shepherd is not going to lose a single sheep.

Golden thought: **"Surely he shall deliver thee."**
"My times are in thy hand: deliver me from the hand of mine enemies, and from them that persecute me" (Ps. 31:15).

August 25

"He shall cover thee with his feathers, and under his wings shalt thou trust: his truth shall be thy shield and buckler" (Ps. 91:4). The psalmist uses an image of the bird covering the chicks with its feathers to convey the truth that God is continually covering the believer with wings of protection. Our best laid plans may often fail, but God never fails in keeping His people. Anything that He allows into our lives is intended for our benefit. The truth of His Word is a great protection from the lies and distortions of the world and the Devil. God's Word turns the light upon our path and our choices. We must search the Scriptures to see that light and to follow the right path.

Golden thought: **"Under his wings shalt thou trust."**
"When I said, My foot slippeth; thy mercy, O Lord, held me up" (Ps. 94:18).

August 26

"Thou shalt not be afraid for the terror by night; nor for the arrow that flieth by day; nor for the pestilence that walketh in darkness; nor for the destruction that wasteth at noonday" (Ps. 91:5–6). The believer should never be afraid because God can never be surprised. He should not be in terror at night because God sees at night also. He should not fear the missiles by day because God knows them also. No pestilence can escape God's notice; no destruction can overpower Him. The believer walks by faith in the keeping power of God. What He allows into the life of a believer is intended for his benefit. The believer should have complete confidence in the wisdom and power of God.

Golden thought: **"Thou shalt not be afraid."**

"Lord, thou hast been our dwelling place in all generations" (Ps. 90:1).

August 27

"A thousand shall fall at thy side, and ten thousand at thy right hand; but it shall not come nigh thee. Only with thine eyes shalt thou behold and see the reward of the wicked" (Ps. 91:7–8). There is no accidental death for the believer in the Lord Jesus Christ. It may look like an accident, but it is really the Lord taking home His child right on time. The Lord sustains His people until they fulfill His purpose for their lives. Unbelievers may be cut off at any time because they do not want God's purpose for their lives. Every believer should walk humbly with God, expecting Him to provide daily protection that he might fulfill God's will for that day. The Lord is leading him home.

Golden thought: **"A thousand shall fall at thy side . . . but it shall not come nigh thee."**

"O keep my soul, and deliver me: let me not be ashamed; for I put my trust in thee" (Ps. 25:20).

August 28

"*B*ecause thou hast made the Lord, which is my refuge, even the most High, thy habitation; there shall no evil befall thee, neither shall any plague come nigh thy dwelling" (Ps. 91:9–10). Dwelling with the Lord permanently is a great protection for the believer. The sense of the Lord's presence is a strength to each saint. If God is our refuge from all harm, difficulties are merely stepping stones down the path of His purpose. We have the sense that God is working all things together for our good. We must not forget His presence or stray from His pathway for us. Each step along the pathway is one step nearer home. Let us walk with Him along our pathway with confidence in His keeping power.

Golden thought: **Because you have made the Lord your habitation, no evil shall befall you.**

"I will say of the Lord, He is my refuge and my fortress: my God; in him will I trust" (Ps. 91:2).

August 29

"For he shall give his angels charge over thee, to keep thee in all thy ways. They shall bear thee up in their hands, lest thou dash thy foot against a stone" (Ps. 91:11–12). Only in heaven will we learn how much the ministry of angels has meant in our lives. We know that they are ministering spirits, sent forth to minister to them who shall be heirs of salvation (Heb. 1:14). But their countless acts of mercy and deliverance will be a source of great thanksgiving in glory. We should give thanks now for what we know is going on, whether we can perceive it or not. God is gracious to His people in sending His servants to attend our pathway.

Golden thought: **"He shall give his angels charge over thee, to keep thee in all thy ways."**

"The angel of God called to Hagar out of heaven, and said unto her, What aileth thee, Hagar? fear not; for God hath heard the voice of the lad" (Gen. 21:17).

August 30

"*T*hou shalt tread upon the lion and adder: the young lion and the dragon shalt thou trample under feet. Because he hath set his love upon me, therefore will I deliver him: I will set him on high, because he hath known my name" (Ps. 91:13–14). By the grace of God the believer can face dangerous adversaries and triumph. The lion, king of beasts, and the adder, a poisonous snake, represent any dangerous adversary. God protects the believer from all harm. Because he has set his love on God, God will deliver him and exalt him. He will set him on high in this world and the next. To know God's name is to understand His Person and to obey His will. God will cause the obedient saint to triumph.

Golden thought: **Because he has set his love upon Me, therefore I will deliver him.**

"What persecutions I endured: but out of them all the Lord delivered me" (II Tim. 3:11).

August 31

"*H*e shall call upon me, and I will answer him: I will be with him in trouble; I will deliver him, and honour him. With long life will I satisfy him, and shew him my salvation" (Ps. 91:15–16). God listens to the prayers of His people. He delights to answer His people and to strengthen them in times of trouble. God will deliver them from all their troubles, some in this life and all in the life to come. He will satisfy His people with life, blessing them for a time in this life and giving them everlasting life in the world to come. God will show His people that salvation means more than endless existence; it means great joy and celebration forever in His presence in paradise. He will satisfy them completely.

Golden thought: **God says, "I will answer him and deliver him."** "Thou art my portion, O Lord: I have said that I would keep thy words" (Ps. 119:57).

September 1

"And shall not God avenge his own elect, which cry day and night unto him, though he bear long with them? I tell you that he will avenge them speedily" (Luke 18:7–8). Believers must never think that God does not hear their prayers, even when the answer is long delayed. The Lord promised that God would avenge His elect. Yet the timing must be left in God's hands. He knows exactly the right time to vindicate the righteous and to condemn the wicked. We should continue praying to Him for deliverance. The righteous have only a short time in which to suffer, but the wicked will have all eternity to weigh their evil deeds. Let us pray with faith, knowing that God will answer right on time.

Golden thought: **God will avenge His elect speedily.**

"Plead my cause, and deliver me: quicken me according to thy word" (Ps. 119:154).

September 2

"For every one that exalteth himself shall be abased; and he that humbleth himself shall be exalted" (Luke 18:14). The proud Pharisee who prayed to himself was ignored by God (Luke 18:11), but the humble publican who begged God for mercy was heard and pardoned by God (Luke 18:13–14). The Lord Jesus thus teaches us all that we should come to God begging Him for forgiveness, cleansing, and mercy. He is pleased to impart such grace to all who ask Him. God is a gracious sovereign who can transform sinners into faithful servants for Him. He intends to use their service, not merely in this life but in the ages to come, in His glorious heavenly kingdom.

Golden thought: **He who humbles himself shall be exalted.**
"Serve the Lord with gladness: come before his presence with singing" (Ps. 100:2).

September 3

"Yea, all kings shall fall down before him: all nations shall serve him. For he shall deliver the needy when he crieth, the poor also, and him that hath no helper" (Ps. 72:11–12). David speaks of the messianic King, who will have universal dominion. Only He can save the souls of the needy (v. 13). The Lord Jesus Christ is the fulfillment of this psalm. "Christ Jesus came into the world to save sinners" (I Tim. 1:15). "According to his mercy he saved us, by the washing of regeneration, and renewing of the Holy Ghost" (Titus 3:5). All sinful people should cry to Him for mercy and forgiveness. "His name shall endure for ever . . . all nations shall call him blessed" (Ps. 72:17).

Golden thought: **He shall deliver the needy when he cries.**
"We shall be saved from wrath through him" (Rom. 5:9).

September 4

"*B*ehold, I stand at the door, and knock: if any man hear my voice, and open the door, I will come in to him, and will sup with him, and he with me" (Rev. 3:20). The Lord Jesus stands at the heart's door and knocks. He will not force His way in. We must open the door and invite Him in. He is ready to meet the needs of every sin-sick soul. His presence removes the lukewarm attitude and imparts to the believer the joy of His salvation. He intends loving fellowship in a banquet of heartfelt celebration. If He is in our heart, we will never be lonely. Let us invite Him in and give Him the best place in the house that His peace may reign in our hearts.

Golden thought: **Jesus says, "I will come in to him, and will sup with him."**

"That Christ may dwell in your hearts by faith; that ye, being rooted and grounded in love, may be able to comprehend . . . the love of Christ" (Eph. 3:17–19).

September 5

"To him that overcometh will I grant to sit with me in my throne, even as I also overcame, and am set down with my Father in his throne" (Rev. 3:21). To the one who conquers by His grace the Lord Jesus Christ will grant the right to sit with Him on His throne. That is a thought of overwhelming grace and privilege. To those who serve Him humbly in this world, He will open the door to increased service and dominion in the world to come. Who knows how vast His program will be in the ages that follow! His people will always be in His presence, always enjoying His love and grace. The thought should strengthen us to stand for Him in this present wicked world.

Golden thought: **To the overcomer I will grant to sit with Me in My throne.**

"Know ye not that we shall judge angels? how much more things that pertain to this life?" (I Cor. 6:3).

September 6

"*B*ut thou, when thou prayest, enter into thy closet, and when thou hast shut thy door, pray to thy Father which is in secret; and thy Father which seeth in secret shall reward thee openly" (Matt. 6:6). The Lord God spurns ostentatious public prayer, but He delights in the soul that seeks Him in private and yearns to fellowship with Him. God is listening and is able to grant the heart's desire of the saint who loves Him. Every saint needs that quiet time of secret prayer and fellowship with God. It is a source of courage and strength to meet life's tests and trials. With God, all things are possible. Without Him, there is nothing that we can accomplish for Him.

Golden thought: **Pray to your Father in secret and He shall reward you.**

"Pray without ceasing" (I Thess. 5:17).

September 7

"*H*e will not suffer thy foot to be moved: he that keepeth thee will not slumber" (Ps. 121:3). God will not permit your foot to slip in the pathway of His will. His grace will keep you steady in your walk for Him. The Lord of all is able to care for each of His sheep. You can walk His pathway with calm trust in His keeping power. The Lord never slumbers: He is constantly alert to every danger that may beset your pathway. Just as the sheep trustingly follow the shepherd, so believers should follow the good Shepherd with confident faith in His guidance and loving care. You may be sure that He will lead you safely home. The fold is prepared and waiting for you.

―――――――――――――

Golden thought: **He will not suffer your foot to slip.**

Jesus said, "I am the good shepherd: the good shepherd giveth his life for the sheep" (John 10:11).

September 8

"Nevertheless I tell you the truth; It is expedient for you that I go away: for if I go not away, the Comforter will not come unto you; but if I depart, I will send him unto you" (John 16:7). The Holy Spirit of God is the Comforter. When the Lord Jesus went back to glory, He sent the Spirit to His people. The Spirit came in power on the day of Pentecost (Acts 2:1–4). Today He still fills the church with His power that believers may be witnesses to the salvation that is in Christ (Acts 1:8). The Spirit empowers the gospel testimony. As the Comforter, the Paraclete, He provides all that the believer needs to serve Christ in this world. We all need to serve and witness in the power of the Spirit of God.

Golden thought: **Jesus said, "I will send Him [the Spirit] unto you."**

"But the fruit of the Spirit is love, joy, peace, longsuffering, gentleness, goodness, faith, meekness, temperance" (Gal. 5:22–23).

September 9

"And when he is come, he will reprove the world of sin, and of righteousness, and of judgment" (John 16:8). The Lord Jesus promises that the Holy Spirit will convict the world of sin because they do not believe on Him (v. 9); and of righteousness because He, the only source of righteousness, returns to the Father (v. 10); and of judgment because if even the Devil will be judged, who else could escape (v. 11)? But the convicting ministry of the Spirit brings men to faith and salvation. Thus, the work of Christ will go forward, even though He returns to His Father. It is our privilege to share the gospel with others and to show them the plan of God's salvation.

Golden thought: **The Spirit will convict the world of sin, righteousness, and judgment.**

"This I say then, Walk in the Spirit, and ye shall not fulfil the lust of the flesh" (Gal. 5:16).

September 10

"*H*owbeit when he, the Spirit of truth, is come, he will guide you into all truth: for he shall not speak of himself; but whatsoever he shall hear, that shall he speak: and he will shew you things to come" (John 16:13). The ministry of the Spirit is to guide God's people into understanding the truth of Scripture. He will reveal the truth of God and will make known prophecies of the future. The overemphasis in some movements on the Spirit is not the will of the Spirit Himself. He leads men to honor the Son, Jesus Christ, and not Himself. We all should submit to His leading and honor Jesus Christ above all. Bringing people to faith in Jesus is the highest task that believers can perform by the power of the Spirit.

Golden thought: **The Spirit will guide you into all truth.**

Paul prays "that the God of our Lord Jesus Christ, the Father of glory, may give unto you the spirit of wisdom and revelation in the knowledge of him" (Eph. 1:17).

September 11

"*H*e [the Spirit] shall glorify me: for he shall receive of mine, and shall show it unto you" (John 16:14). The ministry of the Spirit is to take the revelations of the saving work of Christ to illuminate the minds of believers to perceive how great the salvation is that Christ has secured for His people. He causes believers to honor and serve the Lord Jesus with fuller perception of His greatness. The Spirit does not call attention to Himself; He causes believers to center their lives upon the Lord Jesus Christ. When we yield ourselves most fully to the leading of the Spirit, we will be the best witnesses for the Lord Jesus, leading men to honor Him above all.

Golden thought: **Jesus said, "The Spirit shall glorify me."**
"And because ye are sons, God hath sent forth the Spirit of his Son into your hearts, crying, Abba, Father" (Gal. 4:6).

September 12

"And ye now have sorrow: but I will see you again, and your heart shall rejoice, and your joy no man taketh from you" (John 16:22). The Lord Jesus warns His disciples that they will grieve over the coming crucifixion but assures them that He will rise again. The sufferings of the cross will be followed by the glorious joy of His victory over death. No trial or persecution can remove from the believer his joy in the risen Lord. Our ministry is serving a risen Savior, who can set all men free from the bonds of death. In the light of His resurrection our service should be a joyous testimony to the saving power of the risen Lord. The joy of the Lord is our strength.

Golden thought: **Jesus said, "I will see you again, and your heart shall rejoice."**

"Now the God of hope fill you with all joy and peace in believing, that ye may abound in hope, through the power of the Holy Ghost" (Rom. 15:13).

September 13

"And in that day ye shall ask me nothing. Verily, verily, I say unto you, Whatsoever ye shall ask the Father in my name, he will give it you" (John 16:23). The Father delights in honoring His Son, Jesus Christ. If believers pray in submission to the will of the Lord Jesus, the Father will delight in answering such prayer. The important thing for the believer is to align himself with the will of the Lord Jesus. When we are pleasing Him, the Father loves to grant our petitions. The obedient walk is an important part of intercessory prayer. Day by day we need to be prayer warriors for the Lord Jesus. Have you prayed for the salvation of the lost this day?

_____

Golden thought: **Whatever you ask the Father in Jesus' name He will give to you.**

"The Lord is . . . not willing that any should perish, but that all should come to repentance" (II Pet. 3:9).

September 14

"*H*itherto have ye asked nothing in my name: ask, and ye shall receive, that your joy may be full" (John 16:24). The disciples had not been praying in the name of Jesus, but now the Lord tells them that they should. Now it is our practice to end every prayer with the phrase "in Jesus' name." That is not mere formality. It is instead a recognition that all our prayers are offered to God because of Jesus' intercession on our behalf. He deserves the answer; we do not. Because He died for our sins, we may approach the throne of grace boldly. God is willing to answer prayer because Jesus deserves it. How great is His grace and mercy to us because of Jesus!

Golden thought: **Ask, and you shall receive, that your joy may be full.**

"Pray without ceasing. . . . Brethren, pray for us" (I Thess. 5:17, 25).

September 15

"But the manifestation of the Spirit is given to every man to profit withal" (I Cor. 12:7). The Lord imparts His Holy Spirit to every born again believer. The Spirit gives the believer the assurance that Jesus is Lord (I Cor. 12:3). The Spirit also brings gifts to each believer by which he may serve the Lord in his Christian life. To one He imparts the gift of wisdom, to another knowledge, to others other gifts (I Cor. 12:8–11). The Spirit thus enables believers to serve the Lord and be a blessing to other believers. The Spirit creates a unity within the body of Christ and causes believers to be a benefit to one another (I Cor. 12:12–13). It is a comfort to a believer to know that he does not have to serve in his own strength.

Golden thought: **"The manifestation of the Spirit is given to every man."**

"Let all your things be done with charity [love]" (I Cor. 16:14).

September 16

"*C*hrist hath redeemed us from the curse of the law . . . that the blessing of Abraham might come on the Gentiles through Jesus Christ; that we might receive the promise of the Spirit through faith" (Gal. 3:13–14). The death of Christ upon the cross redeemed believers from the penalty of the law. Now the blessing of Abraham can come to the Gentiles as well. We believe just as Abraham did, that God saves people by faith in His promise. Now we receive the promise of the Spirit, even though we had no heritage of Old Testament revelation. Jesus Christ is the Mediator of all who will believe the promise of God. Praise God for His matchless grace!

Golden thought: **Christ redeemed us from the curse of the law.**
"For ye are all the children of God by faith in Christ Jesus" (Gal. 3:26).

September 17

"*T*he righteous shall flourish like the palm tree: he shall grow like a cedar in Lebanon" (Ps. 92:12). God's blessing rests upon His people. The palm tree is a beautiful illustration. It grows throughout the Middle East. The cedar of Lebanon is one of the largest evergreens in the area. It used to cover the Lebanon mountains, but now it has been cut down until only small remnants remain. But where they can be found, both trees are lovely illustrations of God's blessing upon His people. The righteous will flourish, not merely in this life but also for endless ages in God's prepared place for His people. Even in that glorious place the tree of life will grow and prosper (Rev. 22:2).

Golden thought: **"The righteous shall flourish like the palm tree."**
"It is a good thing to give thanks unto the Lord, and to sing praises unto thy name, O most High" (Ps. 92:1).

September 18

"They hey shall still bring forth fruit in old age; they shall be fat and flourishing" (Ps. 92:14). God's blessing rests upon His people even to old age. An old tree can still bring forth fruit; so can an elderly person bring forth evidence of God's grace. It is an impressive testimony for an older believer to demonstrate faithfulness to God and His Word. The young can learn much by seeing an older saint walking with God and surmounting difficulties with a serene faith in God. The older believer can be a testimony in prayer and consistency that can help the younger in their walk with God. The nearer the saint comes to heaven, the more he should be talking with God.

———————————————

Golden thought: **"They shall still bring forth fruit in old age."**
"Both young men, and maidens; old men, and children: Let them praise the name of the Lord" (Ps. 148:12–13).

September 19

"When thou goest, it shall lead thee; when thou sleepest, it shall keep thee; and when thou awakest, it shall talk with thee" (Prov. 6:22). God's revealed commandments, passed down from one generation to another, are a source of strength and guidance to every believer (v. 20). They lead our steps in the activities of the day; they guard our thoughts at night; and when we awake, they speak to our conscience to impel us in the right direction. "For the commandment is a lamp; and the law is light; and reproofs of instruction are the way of life" (v. 23). God's Word shines like a light upon our pathway, revealing to us the way to walk and please God. _____

Golden thought: **God's Word shall lead us and keep us.**
"Thy word is a lamp unto my feet, and a light unto my path" (Ps. 119:105).

September 20

"*B*ut the mercy of the Lord is from everlasting to everlasting upon them that fear him, and his righteousness unto children's children" (Ps. 103:17). God's eternal mercy rests upon His people, who reverence His name. Faith in God is regularly passed on from one generation to another. Children learn to trust in God because they see their parents and grandparents walking with God daily. The apostle Paul remembered the unfeigned faith of Timothy, "which dwelt first in thy grandmother Lois, and thy mother Eunice" (II Tim. 1:5). He urged Timothy to "keep that which is committed to thy trust" (I Tim. 6:20). We, too, should pass on the faith as a godly heritage.

Golden thought: **The Lord's mercy is everlasting.**
"From a child thou hast known the holy scriptures, which are able to make thee wise unto salvation through faith which is in Christ Jesus" (II Tim. 3:15).

September 21

"Thou sendest forth thy spirit, they are created; and thou renewest the face of the earth. The glory of the Lord shall endure for ever: the Lord shall rejoice in his works" (Ps. 104:30–31). The Lord God sustains all life upon the earth. He created all things and He maintains all things. His glory shall endure forever because He is eternal and will uphold His creation into the ages. This world will pass away, but He has created an eternal home for His people. It will never pass away because He will dwell in the midst of His people (Rev. 22:1–4). No wonder the psalmist says, "I will sing unto the Lord as long as I live" (Ps. 104:33). Let us also sing His praises.

Golden thought: **"The glory of the Lord shall endure for ever."**
"O Lord, how manifold are thy works! in wisdom hast thou made them all: the earth is full of thy riches" (Ps. 104:24).

September 22

"*A*nd this gospel of the kingdom shall be preached in all the world for a witness unto all nations; and then shall the end come" (Matt. 24:14). The Lord prophesied of the future Tribulation period that shall come on all the earth. But even though there will be terrible wars and conflicts on the earth, God's Word shall still be preached. He will have a witness to all nations before the end comes. God's Word is still the power of God unto salvation to all who will believe. This should stir God's people today to get the gospel out that it may work in the hearts of men. God intends that all the world should hear His Word. We should do our part in spreading that gospel of salvation.

Golden thought: **This gospel shall be preached in all the world for a witness.**

"For the life was manifested, and we have seen it, and bear witness, and shew unto you that eternal life, which was with the Father, and was manifested unto us" (I John 1:2).

September 23

"*A*nd hast made us unto our God kings and priests: and we shall reign on the earth" (Rev. 5:10). The four living beings and the twenty-four elders rejoice in the presence of the Lamb in heaven. The Lamb is the Lord Jesus Christ, who takes the scroll, the right to rule, from the hand of the one on the throne. Then these heavenly beings sing His praises because He is extending to them the right to rule the earth. The earth is not to be written off as a lost cause. Mankind has failed miserably to rule the earth for God. But He shall yet rule in power and glory through these redeemed and glorified servants. They shall accomplish His will in ruling the earth to the glory of God. In the end God will win.

_____

Golden thought: **"We shall reign on the earth."**

"Know ye not that we shall judge angels? how much more things that pertain to this life?" (I Cor. 6:3).

September 24

"And the Lord looked upon him, and said, Go in this thy might, and thou shalt save Israel from the hand of the Midianites: have not I sent thee?" (Judg. 6:14). The Lord commanded Gideon to deliver his people from the oppression of the Midianites. Gideon knew that he had no power at all to accomplish this. But the Lord had the power, and all Gideon had to do was to obey the commands of the Lord and to let Him win the victory. We are in the same condition. We have no power to defeat the Devil and win great victories for God. We must obey His Word and let Him win the victories for us. The Lord can use ordinary people to win extraordinary victories for His glory.

Golden thought: **The Lord said, "Go in this thy might, and thou shalt save Israel."**

"But I will sing of thy power; yea, I will sing aloud of thy mercy in the morning: for thou hast been my defense and refuge in the day of trouble" (Ps. 59:16).

September 25

"*F*or whosoever shall give you a cup of water to drink in my name, because ye belong to Christ, verily I say unto you, he shall not lose his reward" (Mark 9:41). This is an unusual promise of the Lord to one who may not be a believer himself but who extends some kindness to a believer just because he belongs to Christ. The Lord promises that there is a distinct reward to that person. This tells us that it is very important to help God's people and be a blessing to them. This certainly applies to believers also, who may go out of their way to help the saints. All the people of God will remember the kindnesses they have received from brethren and will no doubt go out of their way to thank them in glory.

_____

Golden thought: **"He shall not lose his reward."**

"The merciful man doeth good to his own soul" (Prov. 11:17).

September 26

"*Y*et will I leave a remnant, that ye may have some that shall escape the sword among the nations, when ye shall be scattered through the countries" (Ezek. 6:8). The Lord gives a promise to the Jewish remnant. God will bring judgment on the rebellious Israelites, but He will leave a remnant that shall escape the sword. They will be scattered among the nations because of their sins, but God will preserve some. And the day will come when they shall be regathered to the land. God shall breathe upon their dry bones and they shall live again (Ezek. 37:11–14). Israel as a nation shall live to enter the great millennial reign under the blessing of God.

_____

Golden thought: **"Yet will I leave a remnant."**
"And they also, if they abide not still in unbelief, shall be grafted in: for God is able to graft them in again" (Rom. 11:23).

September 27

"*T*herefore thus saith the Lord God; Now will I bring again the captivity of Jacob, and have mercy upon the whole house of Israel, and will be jealous for my holy name" (Ezek. 39:25). God will regather them from their enemies' land (v. 27), and He will pour out His Spirit upon the house of Israel again (v. 29). The restored Jews will rebuild the great millennial temple and worship God from the heart (Ezek. 40–48). At the end of the Millennium God will protect them from a final rebellion (Rev. 20:7–9). God will triumph over all His foes, both on earth and in heaven. He will create a new heaven and a new earth to His glory (Rev. 21:1).

———————————————

Golden thought: **God says, "I will bring again the captivity of Jacob."**

"Now if the fall of them be the riches of the world, and the diminishing of them the riches of the Gentiles; how much more their fulness?" (Rom. 11:12).

September 28

"*H*e [Abraham] staggered not at the promise of God through unbelief; but was strong in faith, giving glory to God; and being fully persuaded that, what he had promised, he was able also to perform" (Rom 4:20–21). Abraham did not consider the extreme age of Sarah or of himself; he centered his attention on the promises of God. He was sure that what the living God had promised, He was fully able to perform. God did keep His promise to Abraham, and Sarah gave birth to Isaac (Gen. 21:1–3). Every believer may take comfort from this account and may learn to trust God more fully. God intends to keep every promise that He makes. God is always true to His Word.

Golden thought: **Abraham was fully persuaded that what God had promised, He was able to perform.**

"And therefore it was imputed to him for righteousness" (Rom. 4:22).

September 29

"Who delivered us from so great a death, and doth deliver: in whom we trust that he will yet deliver us" (II Cor. 1:10). The apostle Paul was a testimony to the faithfulness of God to His promises. He trusted in God, who can even raise the dead (v. 9). Paul surveys three modes of time to demonstrate the faithfulness of God to His promises. God delivered Paul in past time from death; He was continually delivering Paul in the present; and Paul was sure that God would deliver him in the future. The believer should learn from Paul to trust God's promises at all times. Paul had a long life of testimony to God's faithfulness to His promises.

———————————————

Golden thought: **"We trust that He will yet deliver us."**
"For we walk by faith, not by sight" (II Cor. 5:7).

September 30

"*G*ive, and it shall be given unto you; good measure, pressed down, and shaken together, and running over, shall men give into your bosom. For with the same measure that ye mete withal it shall be measured to you again" (Luke 6:38). The believer should be generous in his giving to others because God has given to him with divine fullness. Generous giving moves others to be generous. The person who is stingy in his giving will find that others treat him that way also. But the believer should be generous because God gives generously and not in hope that others will give to him. The Lord encourages a generous spirit because God is generous.

Golden thought: **Give and it shall be given to you.**

"Be ye therefore merciful, as your Father also is merciful" (Luke 6:36).

October 1

"*I*f I take the wings of the morning, and dwell in the uttermost parts of the sea; even there shall thy hand lead me, and thy right hand shall hold me" (Ps. 139:9–10). God is present everywhere. David was sure of His keeping power. He knew that God had made him for an eternal purpose (Ps. 139:13–15). He was satisfied to be in the hand of God and to know that God would fulfill that eternal purpose for his life. Every believer in Christ should have that same trust in Him, that same confidence in His power and purpose. We must all learn to walk with God, as David did. He knew that God would lead him in the way everlasting (Ps. 139:24).

Golden thought: **"Thy right hand shall hold me."**

"How precious also are thy thoughts unto me, O God! how great is the sum of them!" (Ps. 139:17).

October 2

"*T*he eternal God is thy refuge, and underneath are the everlasting arms" (Deut. 33:27). This promise is addressed to the people of Israel, but every believer may apply God's Word to his life and claim the truth of the promises for himself. God sustains every believer. He upholds and strengthens every saint in his walk and service. We need to learn to flee to Him for refuge from every storm and every battle. As we serve, we need to be conscious of the everlasting arms upholding us. The believer should not walk his path with timid trembling but with the faith that God will accomplish His purpose through him and will bring him safely home to Himself.

Golden thought: **"The eternal God is thy refuge."**
"Lord, thou hast been our dwelling place in all generations" (Ps. 90:1).

October 3

"And we know that all things work together for good to them that love God, to them who are the called according to his purpose" (Rom. 8:28). All things are not good, but God weaves together all things to accomplish His good purpose in the life of the believer. All things that come into the life of the believer are intended to help the believer draw closer to God and to walk his pathway with greater trust and zeal. The easy path helps us to rejoice and praise God for His blessings. The hard path causes us to draw closer to the Shepherd and to watch our steps more closely. We need a serene trust in God for every step of the way. Our pathway leads home to Him.

Golden thought: **"All things work together for good to them that love God."**

"Who shall separate us from the love of Christ?" (Rom. 8:35).

October 4

"*B*e strong, O Joshua, son of Josedech, the high priest; and be strong, all ye people of the land, saith the Lord, and work: for I am with you, saith the Lord of hosts" (Hag. 2:4). God gave this promise to the people who were struggling to rebuild the destroyed places in Jerusalem and to reestablish the worship of the Lord. They were a small remnant, but the important thing was that God was with them. He was their protection from adversaries. His protection was going to reestablish the city of Jerusalem. The temple they built was the one the Lord Jesus ministered in. We today need to remember that we cannot win souls or build churches. God must empower our labors for Him. If He is with us, the work will be done.

Golden thought: **"I am with you, saith the Lord of hosts."**

"The desire of all nations shall come: and I will fill this house with glory, saith the Lord of hosts" (Hag. 2:7).

October 5

"For it is written, He shall give his angels charge over thee, to keep thee" (Luke 4:10). In a misuse of a promise (Ps. 91:11), the Devil omits "in all thy ways" and urges the Lord to hurl Himself off a pinnacle of the temple to impress people. The Lord rebuked the Devil by quoting Deuteronomy 6:16, "Ye shall not tempt the Lord thy God." The believer should walk humbly with God, not trying to force God to keep His promises by rash acts. The Lord does have His angels guard our steps, but this is no excuse to act with reckless abandon. The believer serves God best by calm and deliberate service in the clear pathway of His will. His consistent testimony to God will be observed by all.

Golden thought: **"For he shall give his angels charge over thee, to keep thee in all thy ways."**

"Because he hath set his love upon me, therefore will I deliver him" (Ps. 91:14).

October 6

"*E*very good gift and every perfect gift is from above, and cometh down from the Father of lights, with whom is no variableness, neither shadow of turning" (James 1:17). God the Father imparts good gifts, which are unstained by any evil, to His children. He is absolutely unchangeable in His perfect good will. The gracious ministry of the Lord Jesus is a beautiful example of His Father's love and care. We need to cultivate a thankful spirit to God for His constant love and mercy. We need to walk His pathway and use His gifts to the glory of God and for the benefit of others. We also need to develop a consistency of practice in our own spiritual life.

Golden thought: **Every good gift is from above, coming down from the Father.**

"But be ye doers of the word, and not hearers only, deceiving your own selves" (James 1:22).

October 7

"*B*e of good courage, and he shall strengthen your heart, all ye that hope in the Lord" (Ps. 31:24). The believer is not to be faint-hearted, but courageous. He should be bold in living for the Lord and speaking for the Lord. When he is consistent in these virtues, the Lord imparts internal strength to him. If you hope in the Lord, why should you think that He would disappoint your hope? We should trust Him with courage and remain steadfast in our dedication to Him. As we seek to serve Him, He will undergird us with His grace and strength. We should look for opportunities to serve Him and to speak His Word to a world that needs to hear the gospel message.

Golden thought: **"He shall strengthen your heart."**
"Oh how great is thy goodness, which thou hast laid up for them that fear thee!" (Ps. 31:19).

October 8

"*I*f we confess our sins, he is faithful and just to forgive us our sins, and to cleanse us from all unrighteousness" (I John 1:9). If the sinner will confess his sin before God and ask for His forgiveness, the Lord will forgive him and will cleanse him from all his unrighteousness. That is what makes a sinner into a child of God. If we try to excuse ourselves, we merely sink deeper into sin. If you, the reader, have never asked the Lord Jesus Christ to forgive you your sins, now would be a good time to bow your head to ask Him for that forgiveness. Only He can cleanse you from all your sins. Now, let Him lead you into paths of righteousness and service for Him.

Golden thought: **"If we confess our sins, He is faithful . . . to forgive us."**

"If we say that we have not sinned, we make him a liar, and his word is not in us" (I John 1:10).

October 9

"*I* will instruct thee and teach thee in the way which thou shalt go: I will guide thee with mine eye" (Ps. 32:8). This is God's response to David's confession of his sin (vv. 1–5). God is pleased to guide and teach those who repent of their evil ways and seek His face. For those who continue in sin, there is only disaster ahead of them, but for the contrite soul God prepares guidance and blessing. It is vital for the believer to have an open and contrite heart. God delights in teaching those who are quick to respond in obedience. God's guidance extends all the way home to glory. We can walk His pathway with confidence and rejoicing. His pathway leads home.

Golden thought: **God says, "I will guide thee with mine eye."**
"Be glad in the Lord, and rejoice, ye righteous: and shout for joy, all ye that are upright in heart" (Ps. 32:11).

October 10

"And all things, whatsoever ye shall ask in prayer, believing, ye shall receive" (Matt. 21:22). The Lord gave this promise to His disciples, who were plainly living in obedience to the Lord's teaching. All saints who are living in obedience to God's Word should expect God to answer their prayers. There are times in which saints pray unwittingly for things that would harm them. God is wise enough not to give them such things. Sometimes God waits in giving an answer for the very best time. We always tend to think that the answer should be immediate. But for those who wait on the Lord and continue in prayer God will give answers that meet every need. Wait on the Lord.

Golden thought: **Whatever you ask in prayer, believing, you shall receive.**

"Knowing this, that the trying of your faith worketh patience" (James 1:3).

October 11

"*A* faithful man shall abound with blessings: but he that maketh haste to be rich shall not be innocent" (Prov. 28:20). People who want to be rich in material things have failed to put God and His glory above all things in their life. A person who is devoted to God can be content with less than others have. If he has the blessing of God and his needs met, he can be content with very little. But a materialistic society is never content. They always want every new thing that comes along. The believer needs to focus his thoughts on God's Word and on ways in which to please God above all things. If he has God, all other things pale into insignificance. Let us concentrate on being faithful, not on being rich.

———————————

Golden thought: **"A faithful man shall abound with blessings."**
"Moreover it is required in stewards, that a man be found faithful" (I Cor. 4:2).

October 12

"*T*he steps of a good man are ordered by the Lord: and he delighteth in his way" (Ps. 37:23). God rejoices in the path of a good man who is walking in obedience and faithfulness to God's Word. His steps are ordained by the Lord because they are right steps in the right direction. God will uphold and bless those steps. But He cannot rejoice in the steps of a wayward person who has no regard for God's Word. The believer who obeys God's Word should have great confidence in God's ability to lead him in a path of service and blessing that will continue on into all eternity. Providential blessings should not surprise him; trials and difficulties should not discourage him. God will lead him home.

Golden thought: **"The steps of a good man are ordered by the Lord."**

"Though he fall, he shall not be utterly cast down: for the Lord upholdeth him with his hand" (Ps. 37:24).

October 13

"Therefore, my beloved brethren, be ye steadfast, unmoveable, always abounding in the work of the Lord, forasmuch as ye know that your labor is not in vain in the Lord" (I Cor. 15:58). God is omniscient; He knows everything. Because of this the believer should recognize that God knows every inner desire to please Him, every unnoticed deed of service and kindness that the believer has ever done. It does not matter that people do not know about these things. God knows and will manifest His pleasure to the believer throughout endless ages of joy. Let us indeed be steadfast, abounding in labors for the Lord. His pleasure is ultimately the only important thing for the believer.

Golden thought: **You know that your labor is not in vain in the Lord.**

"I know thy works, and thy labour, and thy patience" (Rev. 2:2).

October 14

"And I will give them one heart, and I will put a new spirit within you; and I will take the stony heart out of their flesh, and will give them an heart of flesh: that they may . . . keep mine ordinances, and do them: and they shall be my people, and I will be their God" (Ezek. 11:19–20). God thus promises the Jewish people these blessings in the future kingdom reign. But God has always imparted these blessings to every believer who surrenders to Him and receives His salvation. God changes the inner nature of the believer that he might be sensitive to the voice of God and follow His leading in service and intercession. The believer has a heart devoted to God.

Golden thought: **I will give them one heart and a new spirit within.**

"But now we are delivered from the law, that being dead wherein we were held; that we should serve in newness of spirit, and not in the oldness of the letter" (Rom. 7:6).

October 15

"$\mathcal{H}$e that overcometh, the same shall be clothed in white raiment; and I will not blot out his name out of the book of life, but I will confess his name before my Father, and before his angels" (Rev. 3:5). The Lord promises the true believer that he will be clothed in white raiment, a symbol of the righteousness of Christ, and that his name will not be blotted out of the book of life. He will have eternal life as a redeemed saint. But positively Christ will confess his name before God the Father and the angelic company. Christ will acknowledge him as His faithful servant before all. No higher honor could be given to the believer in that sacred realm.

Golden thought: **"I will confess his name before my Father."**
"They were all filled with the Holy Ghost, and they spake the word of God with boldness" (Acts 4:31).

October 16

"And the work of righteousness shall be peace; and the effect of righteousness quietness and assurance for ever" (Isa. 32:17). The Lord God promises peace and assurance forever. But it will come only by the work of the great King, Messiah. Isaiah prophesies, "Behold, a king shall reign in righteousness, and princes shall rule in judgment" (Isa. 32:1). During the great millennial reign, God's people shall dwell in a peaceable habitation and quiet resting places (Isa. 32:18). Then, the Spirit shall be poured upon them, and the wilderness will become a fruitful field (v. 15). It is no surprise that the great Messiah is called "THE LORD OUR RIGHTEOUSNESS" (Jer. 23:6).

Golden thought: **"The work of righteousness shall be peace."**
"But now in Christ Jesus ye who sometimes were far off are made nigh by the blood of Christ. For he is our peace, who hath made both one" (Eph. 2:13–14).

October 17

"*T*herefore if any man be in Christ, he is a new creature: old things are passed away; behold, all things are become new" (II Cor. 5:17). The person who has been "born again" is a new creation of God. The old nature is still with him, but now he has a new nature that desires the things of God. He has a love for God's Word, the Bible. Prayer seems a natural thing to do. Fellowshiping with God's people is an enjoyment for him. None of these things used to appeal to him, but now they are normal. The new birth has given him a new nature that desires to walk with God and obey His holy Word. The Devil still attacks him, but now he has resources within that enable him to win the victory.

Golden thought: **"If any man be in Christ, he is a new creation."** "Now then we are ambassadors for Christ" (II Cor. 5:20).

October 18

"*F*or his anger endureth but a moment; in his favour is life: weeping may endure for a night, but joy cometh in the morning" (Ps. 30:5). God's anger endures but a moment, for when the believer asks for forgiveness, God forgives. In His favor is everlasting life. We may have sorrows in this life, but they are temporary. Joy comes in the morning. We discover that God has sustained us and carried us through our trials. But in the highest sense joy comes in the morning of His final triumph. He will glorify His people in resurrection power and open up endless ages of opportunity for service and worship. His people shall have joy throughout the ages to come in His presence.

Golden thought: **Joy comes in the morning.**

"And ye now therefore have sorrow: but I will see you again, and your heart shall rejoice, and your joy no man taketh from you" (John 16:22).

October 19

"*G*o ye therefore, and teach all nations . . . teaching them to observe all things whatsoever I have commanded you: and, lo, I am with you alway, even unto the end of the world. Amen." (Matt. 28:19–20). The believer has a clear commission to be a witness to all men about the Lord Jesus Christ. People need to know about His saving power and His sovereign will. But He promises His people that He will be with them all the way to the consummation of the age. He will never desert His people, but He will instead sustain them and empower their testimony to His saving grace. We should joyously make people disciples of Him that they too may have the promise of His everlasting presence.

Golden thought: **I am with you always, even to the end of the world.**

"I will fear no evil: for thou art with me" (Ps. 23:4).

October 20

"*I*t is of the Lord's mercies that we are not consumed, because his compassions fail not. They are new every morning: great is thy faithfulness" (Lam. 3:22–23). Even in the midst of defeat and deportation Jeremiah could remind his people of God's mercy and compassion. We need to remind ourselves that even in the midst of defeat and disappointment, God's compassion never ceases. Great is His faithfulness to His Word. We may call upon Him for help at any time. We need to put ourselves in the place of obedience to His Word, that His blessing may rest upon us. "For the Lord will not cast off for ever" (Lam. 3:31). We need to seek His face for restoration.

Golden thought: **"Great is thy faithfulness."**
"But though he cause grief, yet will he have compassion according to the multitude of his mercies" (Lam. 3:32).

October 21

"*T*he Lord is good unto them that wait for him, to the soul that seeketh him" (Lam. 3:25). Waiting does not come easily for anyone, but the believer must learn to wait on God. We are always in a hurry, but He is not. He always chooses the perfect time in which to accomplish His deliverance. The process of waiting on God and seeking His face is beneficial in itself. He molds us and transforms us as we wait upon Him. The answer to our petitions is often less important than the benefit we receive in continued prayer and fellowship with God. We need to continue seeking Him. The answers to our petitions will come in due time according to His perfect will.

Golden thought: **The Lord is good to them that wait for Him.**
"It is good that a man should both hope and quietly wait for the salvation of the Lord" (Lam. 3:26).

October 22

"*If* any man will do his will, he shall know of the doctrine, whether it be of God, or whether I speak of myself" (John 7:17). Submission of the will to God's will is crucial for every person. If a person is not willing to submit to God, he will never come to a knowledge of the truth. The first step in the knowledge of truth is always surrender to God. When a person surrenders to God, God illuminates his mind and imparts to him spiritual understanding. The Holy Spirit enlightens those who belong to Jesus Christ (I Cor. 2:10). "But the natural man receiveth not the things of the Spirit of God; for they are foolishness unto him: neither can he know them, because they are spiritually discerned" (I Cor. 2:14).

Golden thought: **"If any man will do his will, he shall know of the doctrine."**

"Where is the wise? where is the scribe? where is the disputer of this world? hath not God made foolish the wisdom of this world?" (I Cor. 1:20).

October 23

"*B*lessed are ye, when men shall hate you, and when they shall separate you from their company, and shall reproach you, and cast out your name as evil, for the Son of man's sake. Rejoice ye in that day, and leap for joy: for, behold, your reward is great in heaven: for in the like manner did their fathers unto the prophets" (Luke 6:22–23). Believers should never be discouraged when the world attacks them for testimony to Christ. It is a wonderful privilege to bear reproach for Christ's sake. You are standing with the prophets of God for the truth of God's Word. There is great reward waiting in heaven for all those who bear reproach for Christ's sake.

Golden thought: **"Behold, your reward is great in heaven."**
"Love your enemies, do good to them which hate you" (Luke 6:27).

October 24

"*H*e healeth the broken in heart, and bindeth up their wounds" (Ps. 147:3). God delights in healing the brokenhearted. All those who come to Him for comfort in times of sorrow will find Him to be all-sufficient. He understands the heart need and can impart strength and solace to all who seek His help. No believer should struggle along with sorrow, when the Lord stands ready to lift the burden of sorrow and replace it with the joy of the Lord. We should be quick to cast such burdens onto the Lord and let Him turn them into joyous opportunities for testimony to His grace and love. "The Lord raiseth them that are bowed down" (Ps. 146:8).

Golden thought: **God heals the brokenhearted.**

"Sing unto the Lord with thanksgiving; sing praise upon the harp unto our God" (Ps. 147:7).

October 25

"*F*or it is God which worketh in you both to will and to do of his good pleasure" (Phil. 2:13). God is at work in the life of every believer to mold his will and his practice into obedience to God's Word. The believer who realizes this can yield himself in submission to the Word and let God have His perfect work. God promises that He will keep at the believer until he is perfectly conformed to His good pleasure. At times the believer may prefer a little easier pathway, but God knows exactly what he needs and will bring it into his life for his good. We may rejoice that God has such a high purpose for every believer. We know that we should yield ourselves to His perfect will.

Golden thought: **God works in you to will and to do His good pleasure.**

"Do all things without murmurings and disputings" (Phil. 2:14).

October 26

"*B*e strong and of a good courage, fear not, nor be afraid of them: for the Lord thy God, he it is that doth go with thee; he will not fail thee, nor forsake thee" (Deut. 31:6). Moses reassures the Israelites before they enter the Promised Land that the Lord is guiding them and will fulfill His promises to them. They should not fear the powerful nations that are there because God has promised to give them victory. The believer may well apply this promise to his own Christian life. He faces difficulties and strong foes as well. But God is prepared to guide him and deliver him from all enemies that await him. God will never fail any believer who trusts in Him to keep His promises.

Golden thought: **Be not afraid, for God will go with you.**
"For the Lord knoweth the way of the righteous: but the way of the ungodly shall perish" (Ps. 1:6).

October 27

"At the same time, saith the Lord, will I be the God of all the families of Israel, and they shall be my people. . . . The Lord hath appeared of old unto me, saying, Yea, I have loved thee with an everlasting love: therefore with lovingkindness have I drawn thee" (Jer. 31:1, 3). Jeremiah foretells the promise of the Lord to restore the nation of Israel to their homeland. God has loved His earthly people with an everlasting love. They will yet be restored to the land under His blessing during the millennial reign. The book of Revelation describes the worship in the Jewish temple and the ministry of the two witnesses (Rev. 11:1–4). God will fulfill every one of His promises before the end of time.

Golden thought: **God says, "I have loved thee with an everlasting love."**

"He that scattered Israel will gather him, and keep him, as a shepherd doth his flock" (Jer. 31:10).

October 28

"*I* am the door: by me if any man enter in, he shall be saved, and shall go in and out, and find pasture" (John 10:9). If any person comes to the Lord Jesus Christ for salvation, he will find out that He alone is the door to salvation and heaven. Whenever someone comes to Christ, he will find salvation, deliverance from the guilt of sin; he shall find freedom; he will go in and out; and he will find pasture, sustenance for his spiritual life. Christ is all-sufficient for the believer's spiritual needs. Now, the believer should try to bring others to the Door that he has found. The Lord Jesus came "that they might have life, and that they might have it more abundantly" (John 10:10).

Golden thought: **Jesus said, "I am the door."**
"Then said Jesus unto them again, Verily, verily, I say unto you, I am the door of the sheep" (John 10:7).

October 29

"*L*ooking unto Jesus the author and finisher of our faith; who for the joy that was set before him endured the cross, despising the shame, and is set down on the right hand of the throne of God" (Heb. 12:2). The Lord Jesus Christ Himself is the greatest promise of salvation that the believer has. He is the Author, the one who originated salvation for His people. He came to earth and died for the sins of the world. He is also the finisher, the one who rose from the dead to impart salvation to His people. He will also bring them safely to Himself in glory. Now we should concentrate our attention on Him, lest we be wearied and faint in our minds (v. 3). He is "that great shepherd of the sheep" (Heb. 13:20).

Golden thought: **Jesus is the author and finisher of our faith.**

"Wherefore, holy brethren . . . consider the Apostle and High Priest of our profession, Christ Jesus" (Heb. 3:1).

October 30

"They that sow in tears shall reap in joy. He that goeth forth and weepeth, bearing precious seed, shall doubtless come again with rejoicing, bringing his sheaves with him" (Ps. 126:5–6). Those Christian workers who care enough about the lost to weep for their salvation will surely reap a joyful harvest. Those who go forth with a contrite heart, bearing the precious seed of the Word of God, "shall doubtless come again with rejoicing" (v. 6). There will be a harvest of souls for the Lord. There will be joy both in the witness and in the convert. God's Word will not return void; it will accomplish what He intends. We should sow the seed of the Word for Him.

_____

Golden thought: **"They that sow in tears shall reap in joy."**
"Thy word is truth" (John 17:17).

October 31

"*D*aniel answered in the presence of the king, and said, The secret which the king hath demanded cannot the wise men, the astrologers, the magicians, the soothsayers, shew unto the king; but there is a God in heaven that revealeth secrets, and maketh known to the king Nebuchadnezzar what shall be in the latter days" (Dan. 2:27–28). The practitioners of the black arts cannot tell what God will do in the future, but God reveals His Word to His servants the prophets. Daniel could answer the king because God could reveal to him the whole scope of future empires from the king's time to the end (Dan. 2:37–45). We must trust the promises of the revealed Word of God for the future as well as the present.

Golden thought: **"There is a God in heaven that reveals secrets."**
The king answered, "Of a truth it is, that your God is a God of gods, and a Lord of kings, and a revealer of secrets, seeing thou couldest reveal this secret" (Dan. 2:47).

November 1

"Whosoever shall confess that Jesus is the Son of God, God dwelleth in him, and he in God" (I John 4:15). People who have been saved by the Lord Jesus Christ will confess that He is the divine Son of God. This confession sets them apart from the unbelievers. God the Father is so pleased with this confession of His dear Son that He dwells in the heart of the believer. Now that believer dwells in God, for God fills his life with His presence. His blessing rests upon his pathway, his work, and all that he does. You cannot please the heavenly Father more than by honoring His dear Son. "The Father sent the Son to be the Saviour of the world" (I John 4:14). Believers honor the Father and the Son.

_____

Golden thought: **God dwells in the believer, and he in God.**

"God is love; and he that dwelleth in love dwelleth in God, and God in him" (I John 4:16).

November 2

"For I reckon that the sufferings of this present time are not worthy to be compared with the glory which shall be revealed in us" (Rom. 8:18). God's Word promises that believers are "heirs of God, and joint-heirs with Christ" (Rom. 8:17). We do not see that glory in this present life, but we trust His promise. Present sufferings are but stepping stones to that glorious fulfillment. Believers know that they will need no light from the sun to see the glory of God in that realm to come (Rev. 22:5). We must face our present sufferings with faith and courage, for they will soon be past forever. Let us focus our attention on present opportunities and future glory. God will sustain us through the present suffering.

Golden thought: **Think of the glory that shall be revealed in us.**
"But if we hope for that we see not, then do we with patience wait for it" (Rom. 8:25).

November 3

"Thou shalt hide them in the secret of thy presence from the pride of man: thou shalt keep them secretly in a pavilion from the strife of tongues" (Ps. 31:20). God cares for those who reverence Him. How wonderful to be hidden in the secret of God's presence, even in the midst of prideful men! The believer has a constant relationship with God. The sharp tongues of men cannot harm the peace of God's pavilion for His people. We may rest in His presence whatever the attacks of men may bring. We may pray along with the psalmist, "Make thy face to shine upon thy servant: save me for thy mercies' sake" (Ps. 31:16). God will hear and rescue His servant.

Golden thought: **"Thou shalt hide them in the secret of thy presence."**

"Oh how great is thy goodness, which thou hast laid up for them that fear thee" (Ps. 31:19).

November 4

"Wait on the Lord, and keep his way, and he shall exalt thee to inherit the land: when the wicked are cut off, thou shalt see it" (Ps. 37:34). It is hard to wait, but the believer must wait patiently on the Lord. He does not hurry in accomplishing His will. But if the believer will keep steadfastly in the way of the Lord, he shall see the blessing of the Lord unfold before him. There is an inheritance of joy and spiritual prosperity for the righteous. And even though the wicked seem to triumph again and again, the Lord will cut them off in due time. Everyone must stand before the Lord in the end. Those who wait on the Lord will be exalted.

Golden thought: **Wait on the Lord and He shall exalt you.**

"And now, Lord, what wait I for? my hope is in thee" (Ps. 39:7).

November 5

"*A*nd seek not ye what ye shall eat, or what ye shall drink, neither be ye of doubtful mind. . . . But rather seek ye the kingdom of God; and all these things shall be added unto you" (Luke 12:29, 31). The world focuses on earthly pleasures, but the believer must keep his gaze fixed on the next world. And we must not vacillate back and forth in our interest. Our home is in heaven, not here on earth. We must keep our priorities straight and put the kingdom of God first in our lives. If we do so, we will find out that our heavenly Father is watching over us with care. He will see to it that our needs are met and we are guided carefully into His presence.

Golden thought: **Seek the kingdom of God and all these things shall be added.**

"For where your treasure is, there will your heart be also" (Luke 12:34).

November 6

"*T*rust in the Lord, and do good; so shalt thou dwell in the land, and verily thou shalt be fed" (Ps. 37:3). Every believer should trust in the Lord to sustain him and continue doing good even though it looks as though it will fail. The Lord can see to it that the good succeeds even though it may not look like it. A lost person may turn down the gospel many times before he finally surrenders to it. As the believer trusts in the Lord, He sustains him and opens up avenues of service and testimony. The believer should never worry about whether he will survive. The Lord will see to it that his life counts for Him and that he is preserved, not merely for a few years here but for all eternity.

Golden thought: **Trust in the Lord and you shall be fed.**

"Rest in the Lord, and wait patiently for him" (Ps. 37:7).

November 7

"*B*ut the salvation of the righteous is of the Lord: he is their strength in the time of trouble. And the Lord shall help them, and deliver them" (Ps. 37:39–40). At any time of trouble the believer should turn to the Lord for help. Human resources often fail, but the Lord never fails. Our trust should be in Him, not in things. The Lord is our strength no matter what kind of trouble we may face. But the greatest deliverance the believer can get is deliverance from sin. The Lord is the only one who can accomplish that. We need to turn to the Lord for every trial we may face. The Lord is our Helper. He will never fail His people. Our salvation depends on the Lord, not our own ingenuity.

Golden thought: **The Lord is our strength in time of trouble.**
"For in thee, O Lord, do I hope: thou wilt hear, O Lord my God" (Ps. 38:15).

November 8

"*But* Jesus beheld them, and said unto them, With men this is impossible; but with God all things are possible" (Matt. 19:26). The Lord had said, "It is easier for a camel to go through the eye of a needle, than for a rich man to enter into the kingdom of heaven" (v. 24), and the disciples had exclaimed, "Who then can be saved?" (v. 25). The Lord makes clear that if anyone is saved, it is a supernatural act of God. God must work a transformation in the heart of the unsaved person for him to turn to God for salvation. Believers should praise God for imparting to them His grace and drawing them to Himself through the Lord Jesus Christ. "And let him that is athirst come. And whosoever will, let him take the water of life freely" (Rev. 22:17).

Golden thought: **"With God all things are possible."**
"I can do all things through Christ which strengtheneth me" (Phil. 4:13).

November 9

"*B*e thou faithful unto death, and I will give thee a crown of life" (Rev. 2:10). The Lord Jesus speaks to the persecuted church at Smyrna and reassures them that He understands their suffering. All believers should be faithful unto death; He will give each one a crown of life. He has suffered infinitely more than they have. He will not forget their sufferings. But He counsels those who suffer, "Fear none of those things which thou shalt suffer" (Rev. 2:10). Suffering, accepted in the will of the Lord, only purifies and strengthens the believer. It certainly causes the believer to draw close to the Lord for sustaining grace. We, too, need His grace.

_____

Golden thought: **Be faithful unto death, and I will give you a crown of life.**

"A faithful man shall abound with blessings" (Prov. 28:20)

$\mathcal{N}$ovember 10

"$\mathcal{H}$appy is the man that findeth wisdom, and the man that getteth understanding" (Prov. 3:13). Wisdom is the ability to use knowledge properly according to God's will. The wisdom of God brings happiness because life in the center of God's will is joyous and satisfying. It is better by far than the gain of silver and gold (Prov. 3:14). Wisdom leads to a longer life (Prov. 3:16). The apostle Paul called Christ the wisdom of God (I Cor. 1:24). The believer should seek to attain the true wisdom of God rather than lesser goals. When the believer walks in wisdom, his pathway will be pleasing to God and a blessing to people. That is true happiness.

_____

Golden thought: **Happy is the man that finds wisdom.**

"Wisdom is the principal thing; therefore get wisdom: and with all thy getting get understanding" (Prov. 4:7).

November 11

"When thou liest down, thou shalt not be afraid: yea, thou shalt lie down, and thy sleep shall be sweet" (Prov. 3:24). The person who lives in wisdom and discretion shall find life and grace from God (Prov. 3:21–22). The person who lives wisely in keeping with God's will is not going to stumble in his pathway (v. 23). It is the fool who walks arrogantly, seeking his own advantage at the expense of others (Prov. 1:10–11). But such people lay wait for their own blood (Prov. 1:18). The wicked can expect only desolation (Prov. 3:25). "The curse of the Lord is in the house of the wicked: but he blesseth the habitation of the just" (Prov. 3:33).

Golden thought: **You shall not be afraid; your sleep shall be sweet.**
"But we speak the wisdom of God in a mystery" (I Cor. 2:7).

November 12

"For the Lord shall be thy confidence, and shall keep thy foot from being taken" (Prov. 3:26). The believer must not trust in man, or in his own ability. Our confidence must be in God. He is able to preserve our foot from the snare of the wicked. He can guide us safely through His Word. We need to walk in humble obedience to His Word. "The curse of the Lord is in the house of the wicked: but he blesseth the habitation of the just" (Prov. 3:33). The Lord always acts justly and rewards each person according to his heart attitude. Every believer needs to walk humbly in the pathway of the Lord and trust Him for every step of the way.

Golden thought: **The Lord shall be your confidence.**
"The wise shall inherit glory: but shame shall be the promotion of fools" (Prov. 3:35).

November 13

"He that findeth his life shall lose it: and he that loseth his life for my sake shall find it" (Matt. 10:39). The Lord gives a striking paradox. The person who finds his life in enjoyment of pleasures and the possession of things is really losing his life, for he will have to leave behind all worldly pleasures and possessions. On the other hand, the person who loses his life in the sense of turning his back on the pleasures and possessions of this world for the sake of Christ and His service has not lost a thing. The Lord has prepared endless ages of glorious splendor for His servants that will vastly outweigh all the pleasures of earth. We need to be among those who choose the Lord above all other things in this world.

Golden thought: **He who loses his life for the sake of Christ shall find it.**

"He that taketh not his cross, and followeth after me, is not worthy of me" (Matt. 10:38).

November 14

"For if we have been planted together in the likeness of his death, we shall be also in the likeness of his resurrection" (Rom. 6:5). We who believe on him have been identified with Christ in His death. But the day will come when we shall also be identified with Him in His resurrection glory. Consequently, Paul urges believers to reckon themselves to be dead unto sin, "but alive unto God through Jesus Christ our Lord" (Rom. 6:11). We used to be the slaves of sin (Rom. 6:17), "but now being made free from sin, and become servants to God, ye have your fruit unto holiness, and the end everlasting life" (Rom. 6:22). We should praise God for His glorious salvation.

Golden thought: **We shall be in the likeness of His resurrection.**

"For the wages of sin is death; but the gift of God is eternal life through Jesus Christ our Lord" (Rom. 6:23).

November 15

"*T*rust in him at all times; ye people, pour out your heart before him: God is a refuge for us. Selah" (Ps. 62:8). God's people need to trust in the Lord always. Every day we need His grace and strength. We need to pour out our hearts in fervent prayer to Him. Life is uncertain and dangerous. He is the only safe refuge that we have. The word *Selah* means "think of that." Believers need to ponder the great privilege they have of taking refuge in the God of the universe. How gracious He is to care for His people and to guide them along the path of life to His home for them in heaven. We need to trust in Him every step of the way.

Golden thought: **God is a refuge for us.**

"My soul, wait thou only upon God; for my expectation is from him" (Ps. 62:5).

November 16

"*I*t is vain for you to rise up early, to sit up late, to eat the bread of sorrows: for so he giveth his beloved sleep" (Ps. 127:2). The believer should not try to live the Christian life by sheer grit and desperate struggle. God imparts to His children grace and strength in time of need. We can take our rest without feeling guilty, for God is constantly guarding His own. He imparts to His people sweet rest and strength for a new day's labors. The believer should pace himself with days of faithful, diligent service and nights of serene rest, for God is watching to keep him in perfect peace both day and night. We may trust Him by day and by night.

Golden thought: **God gives His beloved sleep.**

"Except the Lord build the house, they labor in vain that build it: except the Lord keep the city, the watchman waketh but in vain" (Ps. 127:1).

November 17

"*L*et us hold fast the profession of our faith without wavering; (for he is faithful that promised)" (Heb. 10:23). The believer needs to live a strong confession of his faith before men. Day by day he needs to be a testimony to the love and grace of God. His life needs to shine forth in daily obedience to God's holy Word. God is always faithful to fulfill His promises to us. We need to be faithful in living for Him. We need to so live as to propel others toward love and good works for God (v. 24). It is important that we not forsake the assembling of ourselves together (v. 25), for it is then that we can be a help to others by our faithful testimony. God is faithful. Let us not waver.

Golden thought: **God is faithful; let us stand fast.**

"Having therefore, brethren, boldness to enter into the holiest by the blood of Jesus" (Heb. 10:19).

November 18

"As thy days, so shall thy strength be" (Deut. 33:25). The believer should never feel that God is calling him to an impossible task. It is instead a work for which God will supply the guidance and strength that is needed. Each task the believer faces is one the Lord has already planned and is prepared to accomplish through him. Our task is to walk humbly with God and let Him guide our work and direct our path. We need to draw upon Him for wisdom and strength to do a good job for Him. His blessing upon the work means everything. To the end of his earthly life the believer may be sure that God will be with him and will strengthen him for every good work.

Golden thought: **"As thy days, so shall thy strength be."**
Paul prayed, "That he would grant you, according to the riches of his glory, to be strengthened with might by his Spirit in the inner man" (Eph. 3:16).

November 19

"*T*ake that thine is, and go thy way: I will give unto this last, even as unto thee" (Matt. 20:14). In the Lord's parable some who had worked all day felt that they were more valuable and should get greater reward than those who had worked for only an hour. Some old saints fall into that mistake. They think that they are more valuable to the Lord than new converts are. But no one is saved because he is valuable. He is saved because Christ loves him and died for him. In heaven the newest saint is just as saved as the apostle Paul is. Here on earth every believer should serve as best he can in any open door because Christ loves him and not because he is important.

Golden thought: **"I will give to this last, even as unto thee."**
"Humble yourselves in the sight of the Lord, and he shall lift you up" (James 4:10).

November 20

"Oh that men would praise the Lord for his goodness, and for his wonderful works to the children of men. For he satisfieth the longing soul, and filleth the hungry soul with goodness" (Ps. 107:8–9). The Lord deserves the highest praise for His goodness to men. He satisfies the longing soul with the gracious salvation that brings him into fellowship with the Lord Himself. He fills the hungry soul with goodness that transforms him into a servant of God who can satisfy the hunger of others with the bread of life that he has found. We should indeed hunger and thirst for fellowship with our loving God, who has supplied our every need and desires to hear our voice. Let us cry, "Praise the Lord!"

Golden thought: **God satisfies the longing soul and fills the hungry with goodness.**

"O give thanks unto the Lord, for he is good: for his mercy endureth for ever" (Ps. 107:1).

November 21

"*F*or whosoever shall do the will of my Father which is in heaven, the same is my brother, and sister, and mother" (Matt. 12:50). In His public ministry the Lord Jesus showed no favoritism toward His earthly family. He had the great work of salvation to accomplish for all mankind. But when the question arose, He made clear that He had a special bond with the disciples who followed Him. He claimed the believers who followed Him as members of His family. He is gracious in being open to fellowship with anyone who longs for it, and not just special people. That should stir up each of us to a closer walk with the Lord and a better prayer life.

Golden thought: **Jesus said, "Whoever will do the will of My Father is My brother and sister."**

"What, could ye not watch with me one hour?" (Matt. 26:40).

November 22

"*B*ut the meek shall inherit the earth; and shall delight themselves in the abundance of peace" (Ps. 37:11). The arrogant may trample on the meek and make life difficult for them, but God will correct all such abuses. In the end, the meek, who humbly follow the Lord, will inherit the earth. It does not belong to those who arrogantly claim it now. It belongs to the Lord. In the end, He will see to it that the meek inherit the earth. The meek may have little peace now, but they shall have an eternity of perfect peace with the Lord Himself. God keeps His promises and preserves His people. "Wait on the Lord, and keep his way, and he shall exalt thee to inherit the land" (Ps. 37:34).

Golden thought: **"The meek shall inherit the earth."**

"The Lord lifteth up the meek: he casteth the wicked down to the ground" (Ps. 147:6).

November 23

"And whosoever liveth and believeth in me shall never die. Believest thou this?" (John 11:26). Martha was quick to answer Jesus, "Yea, Lord: I believe that thou art the Christ, the Son of God, which should come into the world" (v. 27). It is important for every believer to live his faith and to be ready to confess it before men. The world is ever watching believers to see if they are consistent. The Lord is here promising believers that death does not end it all. Death is the gateway through which believers pass into the presence of God to live with Him forever. The Lord Jesus Christ is the sole Door that leads to heaven (John 10:9). We trust Him for eternal salvation.

Golden thought: **Jesus said, "Whoever believes in Me shall never die."**

"Jesus saith unto him, I am the way, the truth, and the life: no man cometh unto the Father, but by me" (John 14:6).

November 24

"*I* will not leave you comfortless: I will come to you" (John 14:18). The Lord Jesus Christ promises believers that He will not leave them "comfortless," literally *orphans*. God the Father will not leave any believer an orphan. He constantly cares for His children. The Lord Jesus assures us that He will take care of us. His presence is with us constantly. We must cultivate an awareness of Him and learn to talk with Him during the day. The believer can pray anytime during the day or night. The Lord is listening. Practicing the presence of God is an art that the believer needs to learn. Prayer and fellowship with God are a priceless privilege.

Golden thought: **Jesus said, "I will not leave you orphans."**
"Pray without ceasing" (I Thess. 5:17).

November 25

"*For* as the earth bringeth forth her bud, and as the garden causeth the things that are sown in it to spring forth; so the Lord God will cause righteousness and praise to spring forth before all the nations" (Isa. 61:11). The Lord Jesus quoted the first verse of this chapter in His sermon in the synagogue at Nazareth to announce the public ministry that was to follow. But this verse refers to the millennial blessings that will follow the second coming of the Lord. Zion shall be rebuilt and the earth shall bring forth abundant harvests. The greatest blessing will be the righteousness and praise that will be manifest among the nations.

———————————————

Golden thought: **"God will cause righteousness and praise to spring forth."**

"They shall call thee, The city of the Lord, The Zion of the Holy One of Israel" (Isa. 60:14).

November 26

"If thou, Lord, shouldest mark iniquities, O Lord, who shall stand? But there is forgiveness with thee, that thou mayest be feared" (Ps. 130:3–4). This passage assumes that all people are sinners in the sight of God. If God is going to count sins, all the world stands guilty. But God offers forgiveness to those who have reverential trust in Christ. He died upon the cross to rescue us from sin. Those who receive Him find forgiveness and salvation. He changes the whole direction of their lives from selfishness to reverence toward God. Now life can be lived by His grace to the glory of God. His Word is our guidebook homeward.

Golden thought: **"There is forgiveness with thee."**

"I wait for the Lord, my soul doth wait, and in his word do I hope" (Ps. 130:5).

November 27

"And have hope toward God, which they themselves also allow, that there shall be a resurrection of the dead, both of the just and unjust" (Acts 24:15). Christians shared with the Pharisees a hope in the promise of God that there shall be a resurrection, both of the righteous and of the unrighteous. Both the Old Testament and the New record the promise (Dan. 12:2–3; I Cor. 15:12–19), but it is the book of Revelation that gives the most moving portrait (Rev. 22:10–19). The Lord Jesus Christ alone can provide the assurance of a glorious resurrection (John 5:24–29). Faith in Him alone gives assurance of eternal life (John14:6). As Paul phrased it, "Believe on the Lord Jesus Christ, and thou shalt be saved, and thy house" (Acts 16:31).

Golden thought: **"There shall be a resurrection of the dead."**
"We are confident, I say, and willing rather to be absent from the body, and to be present with the Lord" (II Cor. 5:8).

November 28

"*B*ecause thou hast kept the word of my patience, I also will keep thee from the hour of temptation, which shall come upon all the world, to try them that dwell upon the earth" (Rev. 3:10). This promise is often applied prophetically to the last generation before the Tribulation period. The Lord will keep these saints out of the persecution of the last seven years. That may well be correct. Others apply it to any believer who keeps the Word from the heart. That may also be correct. Sometimes the Word is so filled with meaning that more than one application may be ultimately fulfilled. Every believer should draw from this verse the necessity of obeying the Word of Christ at all costs.

Golden thought: **Jesus says, "I will keep thee from the hour of temptation."**

"Behold, I come quickly: hold that fast which thou hast, that no man take thy crown" (Rev. 3:11).

November 29

"*A* man's heart deviseth his way: but the Lord directeth his steps" (Prov. 16:9). People regularly try to plan their way through life. Very often, however, the plans go astray for both mice and men. Our problem is that we cannot know the future. God, however, can foresee future events. He can direct the path of His people so that their steps accomplish His divine purpose. Every believer should trust in the Lord to guide his steps to achieve God's purpose and not just limited human goals. Every believer is important to God. God is prepared to weave the tapestry of life together so that each of His saints achieves His highest purpose in life. Let us put our lives into His hands.

Golden thought: **The Lord directs the believer's steps.**

"Teach me, O Lord, the way of thy statutes; and I shall keep it unto the end" (Ps. 119:33).

November 30

"And he said unto them; Go ye also into the vineyard, and whatsoever is right I will give you" (Matt. 20:4). In the Lord's parable of the laborers in the vineyard the householder represented God and the laborers believers. At the height of harvest the householder hired workers all day long, promising to pay them what was right. They all supposed that those hired early would get a normal wage and those hired later would get less. But the householder gave them all a normal day's wage. When we get to heaven, the humblest believer will get all the glories of heaven that the greatest apostle will. God is gracious and loves to give good gifts to His children. Let us serve Him with zeal.

Golden thought: **God says, "Whatever is right I will give you."**
"Father, I will that they also, whom thou hast given me, be with me where I am; that they may behold my glory, which thou hast given me" (John 17:24).

December 1

"Now of the things which we have spoken this is the sum: We have such an high priest, who is set on the right hand of the throne of the Majesty in the heavens" (Heb. 8:1). Every believer may take comfort in this fact: we have a great high priest, the Lord Jesus Christ, who is constantly interceding for His people. He knows exactly what we need, and He is able to direct the hosts of heaven to accomplish His will. None of us can plead our worthiness, but He is worthy of all. By His own blood He has obtained eternal redemption for us (Heb. 9:12). He is able "to save them to the uttermost that come unto God by him, seeing he ever liveth to make intercession for them" (Heb. 7:25).

Golden thought: **We have such a high priest.**

"Let us therefore come boldly unto the throne of grace, that we may obtain mercy, and find grace to help in time of need" (Heb. 4:16).

December 2

"*F*or every one that asketh receiveth; and he that seeketh findeth; and to him that knocketh it shall be opened" (Matt. 7:8). The Lord Jesus assures believers that prayer is powerful. Every believer who prays in faith will have his prayer answered, not always in ways he expects. But the answer will be more, not less, than he expected. To ask, seek, and knock implies increased intensity. All prayer for increased devotion to God, increased service for God, will be abundantly answered. God delights in manifesting Himself to His people and in opening new doors of service for His people. But we must continue asking, seeking, and knocking. _____

Golden thought: **Everyone who asks receives.**
"Or what man is there of you, whom if his son ask bread, will he give him a stone?" (Matt. 7:9).

December 3

"Then shalt thou delight thyself in the Lord; and I will cause thee to ride upon the high places of the earth" (Isa. 58:14). The Lord promises great blessing upon the restored remnant of Israel. But it is also true that God blesses every saint who walks faithfully in the Lord's pathway. The believer who delights himself in the Lord will find greater blessing in prayer and service than he expected. The Lord draws near those who delight in Him. We must all remember that our highest goal in life must be to please Him, not to achieve our lesser goals. The Lord always honors those who seek His glory and devote themselves to His service.

Golden thought: **I will cause you to ride on the high places of the earth.**

"We love him, because he first loved us" (I John 4:19).

December 4

"*T*he Lord preserveth all them that love him: but all the wicked will he destroy" (Ps. 145:20). The Lord promises to carefully preserve His people. His "great goodness" shall rest upon them (Ps. 145:7). The Lord is full of compassion for His people (Ps. 145:8). They may rest in His keeping power. But He will destroy the wicked, not in the sense of annihilation but in the sense of their losing all that makes life worth living. Loving fellowship with God is something that the saints can look forward to for all eternity. But the wicked have only disappointment, sorrow, pain, and regret to look forward to. There is great motivation for believers to stand fast for the Lord.

Golden thought: **The Lord preserves all them that love Him.**
"All thy works shall praise thee, O Lord; and thy saints shall bless thee" (Ps. 145:10).

December 5

"Take my yoke upon you, and learn of me; for I am meek and lowly in heart: and ye shall find rest for your souls" (Matt. 11:29). The Lord Jesus invites His people to take the yoke of allegiance and service to Him upon them. It is not a burden, but a great blessing. They can give up the burden of grasping for riches, fame, or success and instead live in humble meekness before God, as the Lord Himself did during the public ministry. We do not have to tell others how great we are; let us tell them how great the Lord Jesus is. There is eternal rest in giving Him all the glory and praise. We can walk with Him in serene peace and fruitful service.

———————————

Golden thought: **You shall find rest for your souls.**

"Whatsoever ye do, do all to the glory of God" (I Cor. 10:31).

December 6

"*B*ehold, one like the Son of man came with the clouds of heaven, and came to the Ancient of days, and they brought him near before him. And there was given him dominion, and glory, and a kingdom, that all people, nations, and languages, should serve him: his dominion is an everlasting dominion" (Dan. 7:13–14). The prophet Daniel saw the great Messiah receive the eternal kingdom of God. That will happen when the Lord Jesus Christ returns in glory to set up His kingdom. He will rule in the millennial reign on earth (Rev. 20:4–6) and forever afterwards in the eternal kingdom (Rev. 21:1). It is a privilege for us to serve the great King of heaven.

Golden thought: **"There was given him dominion, and glory, and a kingdom."**
"For he must reign, till he hath put all enemies under his feet" (I Cor. 15:25).

December 7

"*E*ven the Spirit of truth, whom the world cannot receive, because it seeth him not, neither knoweth him: but ye know him; for he dwelleth with you, and shall be in you" (John 14:17). The Holy Spirit of God is the Spirit of truth because He reveals to the believer the true nature of life in the light of eternity with God. In the days of the apostles He was dwelling with the disciples, but after Pentecost (Acts 2:1–4), He is indwelling every believer (Rom. 8:9). It is a precious privilege for believers to have the internal guidance of the Spirit (Rom. 8:14). The fruit of the Spirit is the very character of Christ formed within the believer (Gal. 5:22–23). Paul exhorts, "If we live in the Spirit, let us also walk in the Spirit" (Gal. 5:25).

————————————————

Golden thought: **The Spirit shall be in you.**

"The Spirit itself beareth witness with our spirit, that we are the children of God" (Rom. 8:16).

December 8

"For thus saith the high and lofty One that inhabiteth eternity, whose name is Holy; I dwell in the high and holy place, with him also that is of a contrite and humble spirit, to revive the spirit of the humble, and to revive the heart of the contrite ones" (Isa. 57:15). The eternal, holy God delights in dwelling with people who are contrite and humble. He ignores and resists the proud and arrogant. "The Lord lifteth up the meek: he casteth the wicked down to the ground" (Ps. 147:6). What a blessing that humble saints may dwell with the mighty God forever. They should be continually praising God for the privilege of fellowship with the Almighty.

Golden thought: **God says, "I dwell with him that is of a contrite and humble spirit."**

"In thee do I trust: cause me to know the way wherein I should walk; for I lift up my soul unto thee" (Ps. 143:8).

December 9

"And I heard a voice from heaven saying unto me, Write, Blessed are the dead which die in the Lord from henceforth: Yea, saith the Spirit, that they may rest from their labours; and their works do follow them" (Rev. 14:13). The Spirit reveals that those who know the Lord Jesus as Savior should have no fear of death. Leaving this world means rest from all their labors. But the good that they have done continues bearing fruit. People they have witnessed to get saved; churches they have served grow stronger; their example lingers in the hearts of those who knew them. The lives of God's people may bear fruit for generations to come.

_____

Golden thought: **Blessed are the dead who die in the Lord.**
"The righteous shall be in everlasting remembrance" (Ps. 112:6).

December 10

"Again I say unto you, That if two of you shall agree on earth as touching any thing that they shall ask, it shall be done for them of my Father which is in heaven" (Matt. 18:19). For saints to agree together to pray that God's will be done on earth is a powerful force for good. God is listening and will accomplish His work on earth. But they need to pray in faith and in accordance with God's revealed Word. Only eternity will reveal how much God has done because His people have prayed. Let us persevere in prayer. But let us also remember the prayer meetings in church. Pray for the missionaries in difficult places.

Golden thought: **If two of you shall agree in prayer, it shall be done for you.**

"Brethren, pray for us" (I Thess. 5:25).

December 11

"For the Lord taketh pleasure in his people: he will beautify the meek with salvation" (Ps. 149:4). The salvation of God changes a plain person into a lovely person, a selfish person into a helpful person, a sad person into a joyous person. The meek are those who have surrendered to God to allow Him to use them in whatever way He wishes. God always delights in transforming into something greater than they were. His grace can cause the believer to become a help and a blessing to all he meets. Each believer needs to put himself into the hands of God that He may take and use him to the glory of God and the blessing of others.

Golden thought: **God will beautify the meek with salvation.**

"How beautiful are the feet of them that preach the gospel of peace, and bring glad tidings of good things!" (Rom. 10:15).

December 12

"*H*e will keep the feet of his saints, and the wicked shall be silent in darkness; for by strength shall no man prevail" (I Sam. 2:9). Hannah was not only the mother of a great prophet, Samuel, but her prayer is recorded in Scripture as well. She utters this promise that God will guard the feet of His saints. She had experienced His protection for herself. By mere strength no one prevails; God must allow it. Saints today may trust in God the same way Hannah did. The results will be the same: the blessing of God on the obedient life. But we must be men and women of prayer and trust in God as Hannah was. Who knows what mighty answers to prayer God will work in our lives?

Golden thought: **God will guard the feet of His saints.**

"Except the Lord build the house, they labour in vain that build it: except the Lord keep the city, the watchman waketh but in vain" (Ps. 127:1).

December 13

"Yet the number of the children of Israel shall be as the sand of the sea, which cannot be measured nor numbered; and it shall come to pass, that in the place where it was said unto them, Ye are not my people, there it shall be said unto them, Ye are the sons of the living God" (Hosea 1:10). God is not through with the nation of Israel. The Lord Jesus Christ is coming back to reclaim them as His people. "The Branch of righteousness" shall yet execute judgment and righteousness in the land (Jer. 33:15). The Lord will wipe away tears from all faces and remove the rebuke of His people (Isa. 25:8). "Behold, a king shall reign in righteousness, and princes shall rule in judgment" (Isa. 32:1).

Golden thought: **It shall be said to them, "You are the sons of the living God."**

"And the work of righteousness shall be peace; and the effect of righteousness quietness and assurance for ever" (Isa. 32:17).

December 14

"And I saw a new heaven and a new earth: for the first heaven and the first earth were passed away; and there was no more sea" (Rev. 21:1). John records his vision of the new heaven and new earth. People who have their heart set upon the present earth and stellar heaven will be bitterly disappointed to see all they have hoped for disappear. But John is thrilled to see the beauty and splendor of the new. He notes that there is no more sea, a dangerous part of the present earth. That shows that it is a wholly different kind of earth. He saw the Holy City prepared as a bride for her husband (v. 2). How gracious is God's preparation of His new home for His people—the fulfillment of His promise (John 14:2–3).

Golden thought: **"I saw a new heaven and a new earth."**
"Eye hath not seen, nor ear heard, neither have entered into the heart of man, the things which God hath prepared for them that love him" (I Cor. 2:9).

December 15

"*A*nd I heard a great voice out of heaven saying, Behold, the tabernacle of God is with men, and he will dwell with them, and they shall be his people, and God himself shall be with them, and be their God" (Rev. 21:3). God has always planned to dwell with His people. Sending His Son to redeem them was a step on the way. But He will one day bring them into His presence for eternal fellowship with Him. The whole universe will be made new to celebrate the triumph of God. There will be no barrier between God and mankind. The love and fellowship will be immediate and eternal. Let's praise and thank God even now!

Golden thought: **God Himself shall be with them and be their God.**

"Yea, I have loved thee with an everlasting love: therefore with lovingkindness have I drawn thee" (Jer. 31:3).

December 16

"And God shall wipe away all tears from their eyes; and there shall be no more death, neither sorrow, nor crying, neither shall there be any more pain: for the former things are passed away" (Rev. 21:4). The great voice out of heaven promises that God shall remove from His people all things that cause sorrow, pain, or death. The new heaven and earth shall be absolutely perfect and incorruptible. The people and the angelic beings who will be there will be perfect. Their service and praise for God will be perfect; their joy and fellowship together will be perfect; their understanding of God's plan and purpose will be perfect. They will celebrate the greatness of God and serve Him with joy forever.

Golden thought: **"God shall wipe away all tears."**

"These all died in faith, not having received the promises, but having seen them afar off, and were persuaded of them . . . and confessed that they were strangers and pilgrims on the earth" (Heb. 11:13).

December 17

"*A*nd he said unto me, It is done. I am Alpha and Omega, the beginning and the end. I will give unto him that is athirst of the fountain of the water of life freely" (Rev. 21:6). God is the originator of all things and He will be the consummation of all things. He is prepared to satisfy the thirst of His people with the water of life. There will be no longing that He cannot satisfy completely. The picture of Lazarus in the arms of Abraham is a good representation of the loving reception that God will give His people (Luke 16:22–23). Thirsty souls will be satisfied completely. Only God can satisfy the deepest longings of His people. He will have all eternity to do it.

Golden thought: **God says, "I will give him that is athirst of the water of life freely."**

"Ho, every one that thirsteth, come ye to the waters, and he that hath no money; come ye, buy, and eat; yea, come, buy wine and milk without money and without price" (Isa. 55:1).

December 18

"*H*e that overcometh shall inherit all things; and I will be his God, and he shall be my son" (Rev. 21:7). The true believer in Christ will inherit all the universe. He will be perfectly aligned with God's will. He will be His son, His legal heir. Feminists object to this phraseology, but they forget that women were not legal heirs in the ancient world. John uses the correct word to emphasize the legal right of the believer, man or woman, to be the inheritor of all things through Christ. We can wonder how much authority and responsibility the believer will have in the world to come. It will be a satisfying task for all eternity and to the glory of God.

Golden thought: **He who overcomes shall inherit all things.**
"But the fearful, and unbelieving, and the abominable, and murderers . . . and all liars, shall have their part in the lake which burneth with fire" (Rev. 21:8).

December 19

"And the nations of them which are saved shall walk in the light of it: and the kings of the earth do bring their glory and honour into it" (Rev. 21:24). Some people have the idea that there will be only a few saints in heaven, but Scripture makes clear that there will be multitudes in glory. Many kings have professed faith in the God of the Bible (not just David, Solomon, Asa, Hezekiah, Josiah, and other biblical kings). There will be converts from nations all over the world (Acts 2:9–11). David prophesied of Messiah, "Yea, all kings shall fall down before him: all nations shall serve him" (Ps. 72:11). It will be a majestic worship service.

Golden thought: **The kings of earth bring their glory into heaven.**
"And they shall bring the glory and honour of the nations into it" (Rev. 21:26).

December 20

"*A*nd the gates of it shall not be shut at all by day: for there shall be no night there" (Rev. 21:25). The gates of the heavenly city shall not be shut by day, for the glory of God shining from it would keep all evil away. But there shall be no night there: His glory shall never cease radiating from the city. Now we need night to rest, but there we shall need no rest. Night is the time when fears are greatest and strength is weakest. But there will be neither fear nor weakness in that city. God's glory will shine through every part of it. The city is as clear as crystal; nothing in it can cast a shadow. God is light. His people will shine with His radiance forever.

Golden thought: **"There shall be no night there."**
"Ye are all the children of light, and the children of the day: we are not of the night, nor of darkness" (I Thess. 5:5).

December 21

"*B*ut thou, Bethlehem Ephrata, though thou be little among the thousands of Judah, yet out of thee shall he come forth unto me that is to be ruler in Israel; whose goings forth have been from of old, from everlasting" (Mic. 5:2). The eternal Messiah shall come forth from the little town of Bethlehem. The chief priests and scribes were quick to tell king Herod that (Matt. 2:4–6). The Lord Jesus did not choose to be born in a palace as a pampered child of royalty but in a barn to poor, hard-working people. He understands the plight of the poor and needy and is ready to help them. He promises, "Come unto me, all ye that labour and are heavy laden, and I will give you rest" (Matt. 11:28).

Golden thought: **The Ruler of Israel shall come forth from Bethlehem.**

Pilate said, "Art thou a king then? Jesus answered, Thou sayest that I am a king" (John 18:37).

December 22

"And, behold, thou shalt conceive in thy womb, and bring forth a son, and shalt call his name JESUS. He shall be great, and shall be called the Son of the Highest: and the Lord God shall give unto him the throne of his father David" (Luke 1:31–32). The angel's words to Mary promised the birth of the great Messiah, the Lord Jesus Christ. The words were at the same time a tremendous blessing and a great problem. She was to be the mother of the Messiah, but how could she explain that to others? All believers are citizens of two realms. They need to put the spiritual realm above the worldly and obey God. He can bring great blessing and supply the solution to every problem.

Golden thought: **He shall be called the Son of the Highest.**

"And he shall reign over the house of Jacob for ever; and of his kingdom there shall be no end" (Luke 1:33).

December 23

"And the angel answered and said unto her, The Holy Ghost shall come upon thee, and the power of the Highest shall overshadow thee: therefore also that holy thing which shall be born of thee shall be called the Son of God" (Luke 1:35). The angel explains to Mary the miracle that will take place in her. God is going to incarnate His divine Son in her, and He will be the holy Son of God. Mary surrendered to the Lord's will. "And Mary said, Behold the handmaid of the Lord; be it unto me according to thy word" (Luke 1:38). Simple obedience is always the best pathway for believers. Every believer needs to put himself into the hands of God to let Him work out His perfect will for him. God will do it.

_____

Golden thought: **"The power of the Highest shall overshadow thee."**

"For with God nothing shall be impossible" (Luke 1:37).

December 24

"*A*nd she shall bring forth a son, and thou shalt call his name JESUS: for he shall save his people from their sins" (Matt. 1:21). The name *Jesus* means "Jehovah is salvation." The angel appeared to Joseph, promising that the child of Mary would save His people from their sins. Only the divine Son of God could accomplish such a deliverance. Joseph believed the promise and did everything he could to protect the child and His mother. He later took the child Jesus and His mother to Egypt to protect them from the murderous king Herod (Matt. 2:13–14). The Samaritans recognized that Jesus was "the Christ, the Saviour of the world" (John 4:42).

Golden thought: **Jesus shall save His people from their sins.**
"The Father sent the Son to be the Saviour of the world" (I John 4:14).

December 25

"For unto you is born this day in the city of David a Saviour, which is Christ the Lord. And this shall be a sign unto you; Ye shall find the babe wrapped in swaddling clothes, lying in a manger" (Luke 2:11–12). The promise of the angel to the shepherds caused them to come with haste to find the holy family (Luke 2:16). The shepherds were quick to tell others about the promise of the angel and the celebration of the heavenly host over the birth of the Lord. But Mary hid these things in her heart and pondered them (v. 19). Christ is the Savior of all who will believe in Him. "For by grace are ye saved through faith; and that not of yourselves: it is the gift of God" (Eph. 2:8).

Golden thought: **To you is born this day a Savior, who is Christ the Lord.**

"Christ Jesus came into the world to save sinners; of whom I am chief" (I Tim. 1:15).

December 26

"And there shall be no more curse: but the throne of God and of the Lamb shall be in it; and his servants shall serve him" (Rev. 22:3). Believers do not often consider the effects of the curse upon the earth. There is still beauty on the earth, but nothing like the beauty that will come with the lifting of the curse. But in that celestial city God's servants shall serve Him in the midst of glorious splendor. Before His throne nothing shall detract from the service and worship of God. Heaven is not a place of idleness but of continuous work that is satisfying, not tiring. There will not be one bored person in glory. Every saint will be active and rejoicing in everything that he does.

Golden thought: **"His servants shall serve him."**
"Wherefore we receiving a kingdom which cannot be moved, let us have grace, whereby we may serve God acceptably with reverence and godly fear" (Heb. 12:28).

December 27

"And they shall see his face; and his name shall be in their foreheads. And there shall be no night there; and they need no candle, neither light of the sun; for the Lord God giveth them light: and they shall reign for ever and ever" (Rev. 22:4–5). To see God face to face is the transforming vision. His character shall be stamped upon their visage. There can be no night, for the glory of God shines through everything. They need no sun, for God's glory is shining through them. They shall reign forever: His glory impels them to influence the universe for good. Who knows the magnificent plans that the Lord has for the universe to come! And His servants will be His agents of grace and glory.

Golden thought: **"They shall see his face . . . and they shall reign for ever."**

"If we suffer, we shall also reign with him" (II Tim. 2:12).

December 28

"*B*ehold, I come quickly. . . . And, behold, I come quickly; and my reward is with me, to give every man according as his work shall be" (Rev. 22:7, 12). The Lord Jesus repeated the promise for emphasis. His coming is something we look forward to and must be ready for. When He comes, He will give rewards to His faithful servants. Now we should be diligent in our service, looking for ways in which we can further the work of the Lord. We must not waste our time or our opportunities. The servant who was faithful with five talents did not lose them but rather gained much more to use still further (Matt. 25:20–21).

Golden thought: **Jesus says, "I come quickly; and my reward is with me."**

"His lord said unto him, Well done, thou good and faithful servant: thou hast been faithful over a few things, I will make thee ruler over many things" (Matt. 25:21).

December 29

"*F*or I testify unto every man that heareth the words of the prophecy of this book, If any man shall add unto these things, God shall add unto him the plagues that are written in this book" (Rev. 22:18). No man can add to the prophecies or the promises of God. He alone has the power and authority to fulfill them. By faith we receive them and seek to fulfill them as He wills. God has put everything into Scripture that we need to know. We must search the Scriptures and obey what we see in them. We must hear His Word with submission. One thing we know is that His will is to invite the lost to come to Jesus. "Let him that heareth say, Come" (Rev. 22:17).

Golden thought: **If any man add to these things, God shall add plagues to him.**

"With my whole heart have I sought thee: O let me not wander from thy commandments" (Ps. 119:10).

December 30

"And if any man shall take away from the words of the book of this prophecy, God shall take away his part out of the book of life, and out of the holy city, and from the things which are written in this book" (Rev. 22:19). The promises of God are sure to those who trust in His Word. But if anyone wishes to delete what God has promised will happen, God will delete him from the Book of Life. God takes His Word very seriously; we should also. To have one's name in the Book of Life, to have a part in the Holy City, will be the pinnacle of joy and delightful fellowship in the life to come. To forfeit that is tragedy. The wicked do not know what they will miss.

———————————

Golden thought: **To have a part in the Book of Life and the Holy City is joy forever.**

"My soul fainteth for thy salvation: but I hope in thy word" (Ps. 119:81).

December 31

"The Lord's last promise is "Surely I come quickly" (Rev. 22:20). It is the third time in this context that He has promised to come quickly (Rev. 22:7, 12). We need to be spiritually alert, looking for that blessed hope that the apostle Paul described (I Thess. 4:13–18). "The Lord himself shall descend from heaven with a shout, with the voice of the archangel, and with the trump of God: and the dead in Christ shall rise first: then we which are alive and remain shall be caught up together with them in the clouds to meet the Lord in the air: and so shall we ever be with the Lord" (I Thess. 4:16–17). We need to be ready to meet Him every moment. _____

Golden thought: **God gives special promises to His people. We need to look for them.**

"Because thou hast made the Lord, which is my refuge, even the most High, thy habitation; there shall no evil befall thee" (Ps. 91:9–10).

Stewart Custer acquired a love for learning as a little boy. He writes **God's Promises New Every Day** as a man whose capacity to know and share the Lord have, by grace, come to a sweet fruition. He and his wife, Carol, have been married for forty-five years, and he is senior pastor of Trinity Bible Church in Greenville, South Carolina, where he has served for over twenty years.